"Larry Crabb once again proves himself to be the teacher of our inner life. I live more richly because of the PAPA prayer. You will too."

—*Bob Buford/Founder of Leadership Network*

"Spirituality is a hot topic right now, and Larry Crabb has addressed the essence of spirituality in this book. Prayer that negotiates intimacy with God is what spirituality is all about, and Larry helps us to do just that."

—*Tony Campolo/Professor Emeritus at Eastern University*

"In *The PAPA Prayer*, Larry gives us, not a formula, but a wonderfully biblical and intimate form for our prayer lives. It not only encourages us to come to the Father through prayer, it also opens the door to the staggering possibilities of receiving, not what we want, but what He longs to give."

—*Michael Card/Music Artist, Author, and Bible Teacher*

"We're too busy, too preoccupied, and certainly far too easily pleased when it comes to our relationship with God. If your prayers feel empty and God feels distant, and yet your heart still cries out to know Him, you have come to the right place. Larry takes you on an exhilarating, passionate ride to embrace and know God like you never have before."

—*Tim Clinton/President of the American Association of Christian Counselors*

"In *The PAPA Prayer*, Larry Crabb continues his journey to understand and enter into a real relationship with God. This time, he seeks to guide us into a truthful, candid way to pray and be with God who is neither silent nor stern but longing for us to lean into Him as our Papa."

—*John Coe/Director of the Institute for Spiritual Formation at Talbot School of Theology*

"Larry Crabb unlocks the key to genuine prayer ... relationship with the living God. His insight about the state ... t on target. Don't miss his soul-searching appeal in ...

—*T... ...rsity*

"For as long as I've been a Christian, let alone ... with how I pray. . . . Although the PAPA approach is a radical shift away from how I've always prayed, I believe it is much, much closer to how my heavenly Father longs for me to relate to Him."

—*Rev. Dr. Ken Fong/Evergreen Baptist Church of LA*

"Anything that gets us to praying is good. In *The PAPA Prayer*, Larry Crabb goes much further and outlines the right way to pray. It's a book that will turn praying right-side-up"

—*Steve Green/Music Artist*

"Larry Crabb does more than anyone I know to help us accurately discern and sensitively apply the root principles of healthy relationships. Here, he points the way for all relational health to find its fountainhead in the ultimate relationship—with our Eternal Papa."

—*Jack W. Hayford/President of the International Foursquare Church and Chancellor of The King's College and Seminary*

"I'm thankful for this book. I suspect that God is far more thankful—thankful like a tired father is thankful to get his preschoolers past the candy aisle at Wal-Mart. I suspect He's thankful for someone who would help His children speak their deepest desire, forget the candy, and know their Father. Our Papa is sweeter, richer, better than any candy this world has to offer. With practical advice and helpful examples, Larry coaxes us into our Father's lap, where we lose ourselves and find ourselves in Him."

—*Peter Hiett/Senior Pastor of Lookout Mountain Community Church*

"The disciples said to Jesus Christ, 'Lord, teach us to pray.' And so we—2,000 years later—also would say, 'Lord, teach us to pray.' This book helps to answer that prayer."

—Dr. James Kennedy/Senior Minister of Coral Ridge Presbyterian Church and Chancellor of Knox Theological Seminary

"I generally read books to stimulate my mind, but I read this one for my soul, and it has left an imprint that I believe will be with me for the rest of my life. In these pages you will be introduced to a new way of praying that will, I guarantee, change the way you think about prayer; and, best of all, you will actually be motivated to pray continually, joyfully, and purposefully. This is a book for all of us who want to pray more but don't; for all of us who have been discouraged because our prayers have not been answered, and for those of us whose priorities in praying need to be re-directed. It is also for those who have read many books on prayer and think they need not read another one! Read these pages and let God change your perspective and your heart."

—Erwin Lutzer/Senior Pastor of The Moody Church

"We've come to expect that, with regularity, Larry Crabb will offer us all fresh insights on some core issue of our Christian journey. Now comes *The PAPA Prayer* with its refreshing, insightful approach to the core issue of connecting with God. Among the many books written on the subject of prayer, Larry offers us a standout contribution in our effort to strengthen our prayer lives and our ability to hear God speak into our daily experience."

—Gordon MacDonald/Author

"The movement in Larry's heart from 'I should pray' to 'I want to pray' is the revolutionary result of fidelity to *The PAPA Prayer*, an awesome gift and a sterling book."

—Brennan Manning/Author

"Are you tired of prayer formulas that don't fit real life? Have you grown disillusioned with prayer, and perhaps with God? In his new and perhaps most hopeful book yet, Larry Crabb introduces us to relational prayer—an approach to prayer beyond formulas. These are seasoned insights from an honest man of faith."

—Brian McLaren/Author and Activist (anewkindofchristian.com)

"Larry Crabb has a gift of bringing new perspectives to time-honored concepts. Perhaps nothing is more time-honored than prayer, and once again Crabb inspires us to think anew, to engage in a living faith that bypasses clichés and formulas. This is a book for all who yearn to know and be known by God."

—Mark R. McMinn/Professor and Author

"While Larry humbly refers to himself as an 'ecstatic first grader' in God's school of prayer, he writes with his typically keen insight, synthesis, and wisdom and produces a book that will be for so many truly revolutionary. If your prayer life has become dull and confusing, dive into *The PAPA Prayer*. You'll learn that prayer is not about asking. It's about relationship, dialogue, and learning to fall in love with God. The true center of prayer is abiding in and experiencing corelationship with your real Papa."

—Gary W. Moon/Author, Professor, and Vice President for Spiritual Development at the Psychological Studies Institute

"I've been perplexed, disappointed, angry, and at times nearly hopeless because of 'unanswered' prayer. *The PAPA Prayer* has pointed me to a new way to pray and live, centered on listening to God before I make requests of God. If you have struggled with prayer as I have, you will want this book!"

—Evan Morgan/President of Christian University GlobalNet

"Trust me, this is not just another book on prayer. It's a paradigm shift that just might change how you understand your relationship with Christ and the role of prayer in that relationship. Larry's distinction between a narcissistic, false prayer and Christ-centered, true prayer alone is worth the price of the book. This isn't just theory. Larry provides a practical and doable Four-Day Plan that will let you try the PAPA prayer on for size. This is one of the most practical books Larry has written. You may never look at prayer the same again."

—*Gary Oliver/Executive Director of The Center for Relationship Enrichment and Professor of Psychology and Practical Theology at John Brown University*

"Dallas Willard said once that prayer, at its core, is 'talking to God about what we're doing together.' In this book, Larry Crabb is our honest, humble, eager, thoughtful guide."

—*John Ortberg/Teaching Pastor of Menlo Park Presbyterian Church*

"Here is a searchingly realistic exploration of what it means for the person that is really you to meet with the real God in real, God-centered prayer and communion. Larry Crabb is a Christian adventurer, always in pursuit of human and spiritual reality, and this latest communiqué from the world of his [inner] travels is surely his most powerful book yet."

—*J. I. Packer/Professor of Theology at Regent College*

"In chapter one of *The PAPA Prayer*, Larry Crabb promises the reader a relational prayer journey that 'will carry you into a heavenly reality.' Does the rest of his book make good on that promise? I would encourage you to 'come and see.' If you feel that your prayers are like shooting blanks, the PAPA prayer will enable you to repair your way to the solution. The spiritual lessons in this book are invaluable; the experience it yields is indispensable."

—*Chuck Smith Jr./Author*

"Longing for a deeper, more 'direct connect' with God? Larry Crabb wants to take you there! This read will shatter your view of prayer as it used to be and welcome you to the satisfying joy of relational communion with 'The One' who is waiting to hear from you."

—*Dr. Joseph M. Stowell/Teaching Pastor of Harvest Bible Chapel*

"In *The PAPA Prayer*, Larry Crabb writes deeply yet clearly about the crucial importance of putting relational prayer before petitionary prayer: presenting, attending, purging, and approaching prayer that enables us to relate intimately with God. This is a profound book that will transform your prayer life and deepen your relationship with God. It will help you get God before praying to get things from God!"

—*Siang-Yan Tan/Senior Pastor and Professor of Psychology at Fuller Theological Seminary*

"Few activities bring more meaning to our lives than prayer, yet there is much we still do not understand about it. Larry Crabb brings both a depth of understanding, as well as usable and practical steps, to living out a relationship with God that is based on true prayer."

—*John Townsend/Author and Psychologist*

"*The PAPA Prayer* is deceptively simple, yet profoundly real. I learned and grew as I read these liberating truths."

—*Jerry E. White, PhD, president emeritus, The Navigators*

"Larry Crabb's *PAPA Prayer* will certainly clear the obstacles to God being with us as He intended, in the conversational relationship that is the eternal kind of life."

—*Dallas Willard, best-selling author of* The Divine Conspiracy

CR

To my
four grandchildren
(as of 2005)
Josie, Jake, Kaitlyn, Keira

May the PAPA prayer
lead you into the arms of God

THE
PAPA
PRAYER

The prayer you've never prayed

LARRY CRABB

THOMAS NELSON
Since 1798

NASHVILLE DALLAS MEXICO CITY RIO DE JANEIRO

THE PAPA PRAYER

© 2006 by Larry Crabb.

Published in Nashville, Tennessee, by Thomas Nelson.
Thomas Nelson is a trademark of Thomas Nelson, Inc.

Thomas Nelson, Inc. titles may be purchased in bulk for educational, business,
fund-raising, or sales promotional use. For information, please e-mail
SpecialMarkets@ThomasNelson.com.

Published in association with Yates & Yates, LLP, Attorneys and Counselors, Orange,
California.

Some names and details have been changed to respect the privacy of people whose personal
stories are shared in this book.

Unless otherwise indicated, Scripture quotations are taken from The Holy Bible, New
International Version® (NIV®). © 1973, 1978, 1984 by International Bible Society. Used by
permission of Zondervan. All rights reserved. Scripture quotations marked (MSG) are taken
from *The Message* by Eugene H. Peterson. © 1993, 1994, 1995, 1996, 2000, 2001, 2002.
Used by permission of NavPress Publishing Group. All rights reserved. Scripture quotations
marked (KJV) are taken from the King James Version of the Bible. Public domain.

Cover Design: The Office of Bill Chiaravalle | www.officeofbc.com
Cover Photo: The Image Bank / Chris Close
Interior Design: Inside Out Design & Typesetting

Library of Congress Cataloging-in-Publication Data
Crabb, Lawrence J.
The Papa prayer: discover the sound of your father's voice / by Larry Crabb.
    p. cm.
    Summary: "A revolutionary conversational approach to talking with and enjoying God"—
Provided by publisher.
    Includes bibliographical references.

    ISBN 978-1-59145-424-3 (hardcover)
    ISBN 978-1-59145-460-1 (international paperback)
    ISBN 978-0-7852-8917-3 (trade paper)

1. Prayer—Christianity.   I. Title.

BV210.3.C73 2006
248.3'2—dc22   2005032043

Printed in the United States of America
10 11 12 RRD 15 14 13

But if God is so good as you represent Him,
and if He knows all that we need, and better far than we do
ourselves, why should it be necessary to ask Him for anything?

I answer, What if He knows Prayer to be the thing we need first
and most? What if the main object in God's idea of prayer be the
supplying of our great, our endless need—the need of Himself?
Hunger may drive the runaway child home, and he may or may
not be fed at once, but he needs his mother more than his dinner.
Communion with God is the one need of the soul beyond all other
need: prayer is the beginning of that communion, and some need is
the motive of that prayer. So begins a communion, a talking with
God, a coming-to-one with Him, which is the sole end of prayer.

GEORGE MacDONALD

contents

Part 2: Learning to Pray the PAPA Prayer

Practical Helps for Learning to Pray the PAPA Prayer

Acknowledgments

*U*nless you stand on the shoulders of giants, you will not see very far. If I've seen anything of value regarding prayer, credit goes to spiritual giants, most of them now in heaven, some still here, for whom prayer was first communion, then petition.

And unless you live in spiritual community, you won't get much done, at least not much of spiritual value. So—

- Thanks to Joey Paul for believing I had something to say about prayer and then doing all he could to help me say it well.

- Thanks to all Joey's colleagues at Integrity for long meetings, dedicated effort, and talented thought that encouraged me to keep writing.

- Thanks, as always, to Sealy Yates (and Jeana) for caringly shepherding the bumpy process of moving a book from an idea to reality.

- Thanks to my spiritual formation group for warmly enduring my start-and-stop experiments in moving closer to God.

- Thanks to my incredible NewWay Ministries team—Kep, Claudia, Andi, Jim, Trip, and Maribeth for your passionate support.

- Thanks to Marcia and Randy for faithful prayers and invaluable wisdom.

- Thanks to friends who let me tell a little of their stories in this book.

- Thanks to Trip, Glen, Tim, Ken, Evan, Jimmy, and Kent for deep friendship and insightful conversations along the way of writing about prayer (and special thanks to Trip for typing hundreds of faxed scribble-filled pages).

- Thanks to Kim and Lesley for great feedback on the manuscript.

- Last but first, thanks to Rachael for staying present during wild mood swings, preoccupied absences, and confusingly expressed confusion as I wrote this book. You really are the most remarkable woman I know.

Three Stories

I picked up a good friend this morning at eleven o'clock. We were going to run a few errands and then grab some lunch. I invited him along because I wanted to be with him. I like his company.

I told him I was writing a book on prayer.

"What's your big idea?" he asked.

"Well, as I've always said, prayer is the weakest part of my Christian life. I've read stories about great men of prayer, like George Müller, and wondered what I was doing wrong. It's just recently become clear to me that my prayer life has been mostly about trying to get God to do something for me. That never seemed wrong before."

He was still listening, so I continued. "I've read books that say prayer is an opportunity to have a conversation with God, like two good friends getting to know each other better. And that never made sense to me.

"But it does now. I really believe God has given me what I call the PAPA prayer as a way to get so close to God that He actually lives His life through me. And that idea is very different from trying to control God or persuade Him to do certain things for me. Prayer now feels less about asking for something and more about enjoying someone. As I get to know God better and learn to trust His good intentions toward me, what I desire most falls more into line with what He desires, and I end up asking for what I know we both want. So I thought I'd write about what I now understand prayer to be."

My friend turned toward me and said, "Suppose when you picked me up, the first thing I said to you had been, 'Larry, I need you to come by our house tonight. Mary and I need your advice about something. And could you run by the drugstore? I need to pick up a prescription.' When we sit down for lunch, I ask you about one of my kids. 'And oh, by the way, any chance of a loan? Things have been pretty tight. To be honest with you, I'm hoping you'll pick up lunch, if that's OK.'"

He continued, "How would you feel if I talked to you like that? Yet that's how I talk to God. As you were telling me about your book, that just popped into my mind. I'd never do that to you. I like just being with you. But I don't know how to just be with God. So I ask Him for lots of things. Is your book going to talk about why I do that and how I can be with God?"

I replied, "I'm going to begin the book with everything you just said."

❖   ❖   ❖

I called a close friend earlier this evening. Six months ago, her husband left her. When she heard my voice, she said, "Hey, good to hear from you. What have you been up to?"

I told her I was writing a book on prayer.

She replied quickly, "Send me the first copy. I've never been more confused about prayer in my life. Until the divorce, I prayed all the time. As long as life was going reasonably well, I figured God was answering my prayers. And what wasn't changing I still prayed about. I never saw how demanding I was with God. All I wanted from Him was to change this or change that. I never saw what I was doing. I really thought I was trusting God.

"Then everything fell apart. Now I don't even want to pray like I used to. What I want now is to have a real conversation with God, where I experience Him and hear His voice and feel His strength. I want so badly to feel like I'm talking to God and He's talking to me, like two friends enjoying each other rather than me trotting out my wish list. Does what I'm saying fit with what you're going to write about?"

I replied, "Sounds like you've been reading my mind."

❖ ❖ ❖

Brennan Manning and I were chatting after we had spoken at a conference together.

"Where are you heading from here?" I asked.

"I begin a weeklong prayer retreat by myself in two days."

I'd never done that, so I was curious. "What does a week like that do for you? How does God respond to your praying for a week?"

Brennan looked a little puzzled, and then said, "I've never thought about what I get out of it. I just figure God likes it when I show up."

an invitation to pray

≈

The PAPA Prayer

This book is for people who long to hear God's voice, who want to know God so well that His life actually becomes theirs.

Let me ask you nine questions to see if this describes you:

1. Ever ask for something from God that you didn't receive?
2. Ever pray for guidance, especially in a difficult relationship, that never came?
3. Ever really need to hear God's voice and then try to believe you did, even though you weren't sure?

My answer is yes to all three questions. What's yours? Here are a few more:

4. Do you sometimes feel that God is turning a deaf ear to your most desperate prayer requests?
5. Have you ever prayed for comfort yet ended up feeling more empty and alone after you prayed?
6. Has praying for strength to overcome temptation ever left you feeling just as weak and the temptation just as strong, or even stronger?

How did you answer these questions? I answered yes. The three final questions reach a little deeper:

7. Do you know God well enough to enjoy His company, the same way you enjoy being with a family member or close friend?
8. Do you want to know God better and enjoy Him more than you know and enjoy anyone else?
9. Do you connect with God in such a way that enables you to hear His voice and to know He's right there with you?

For years, I've wished I could answer yes to those final three questions. But I've had to say no.

Perhaps that's been your answer as well. Like me, you've been caught up with just keeping on top of things—paying bills, arranging carpools, getting through another day at work or doing another load of laundry, squeezing in time for yourself, handling family tensions, and dealing with all the emotions you feel but admit to no one. Through it all, you try to experience some sense of God, try to believe that your life means something in some invisible big scheme of things. But you have no energy left over to worry about the quality of your relationship with God.

Enjoy Him? Get to know Him better? Hear His voice? Yeah, right. You can barely find a couple of minutes to read the Bible every morning. Truth is, even when you do, your "time with God" doesn't mean much. It's dry. And you're bored.

An eminent but unnamed Christian once confided to a close friend, "When I go to prayer, I find my heart so loath to go to God, and when it is with Him, so loath to stay."[1]

If, like so many, you're busy with life and confused about prayer, the odds are that your prayers have pretty much consisted of one-liner pleas for help: "God, keep me from blowing up at my kid." "God, let the dentist find nothing more to drill." "God, don't let this deal fall through." "God, let my wife's plane land safely."

For a long time now, without even realizing it, you've seen God as an ally in your purposes. You've lost sight of the fact that He sees you as an ally in His. "God, give me the life I want" has been the theme of your prayers. But now you can hear the muffled cry coming from the center of your heart: "God, let me know You better." And you know that's a very different prayer.

The frantic pace of life, coupled with a heavy sense of deadness beneath everything you do, has left you knowing you were built for more. You're hungry. You know your hunger has more to do with knowing God better than with getting more blessings from Him. You long to connect with Him so closely that you hear His voice as clearly as a child lost in the woods hears her daddy call her name.

If you can sense these yearnings stirring in your heart, then this book is written to you. I've written it from my heart to yours. I'm on the same journey.

For years, I've prayed as if the real purpose of prayer were to get the things I want from God. And I thought those things were the obvious blessings of life, the things we all want that make our lives happier, more meaningful and satisfying. But I'm coming to see that what I most want is Him. I want to know Him, trust Him, hear His voice, and experience His power to live the way He tells me to, whether things go my way or not. That, I'm discovering, gives me a kind of solid joy nothing else provides.

With a quiet excitement I've rarely known, I can say that the Holy Spirit through the Bible has led me into a new way to pray that is bringing me to another level of closeness with God.

Scores of Christians over the centuries have recognized the revolutionary secret of prayer that I will tell you about in this book. It's been in the Bible all along. I'm just now discovering it.

And as I pray this new way, streams of living water I've only read about before, and for years have longed to taste, are now flowing into the desert of my soul. Some days it's only a trickle. Some days are still dry.

But I now know what it is to splash like a child in cool water where once there was only hot sand. Paul could sing while in jail. He knew a source of joy that had nothing to do with the blessings of life. And he knew that we, too, could experience that joy whether our son sells drugs or leads a Bible study, whether we just lost our job or inherited a million dollars, whether our days seem pointless or full of purpose. We'll hurt, but we can sing.

If you're familiar with my books or if you've heard me speak, you know I'm a relentless realist. You know I'm not given to spiritual exaggeration. I don't claim to see light when I'm stuck in a cave. I don't claim to feel God's presence when I don't. I don't fake excitement or joy. When I'm miserable, I'm miserable. I don't try to hide it—or when I do, I'm not terribly successful.

But something is happening. It feels new. I know it's good. It's deep. And it's real. And it's happening through prayer. If you've been secretly wondering what prayer is all about, if you long to get close enough to God to hear His voice, then this book could be life changing for you.

This book is all about a way to pray, a way to talk to God a little and listen to God a lot, a way to get better acquainted with God—and yourself—through a special kind of two-way conversation, a way to pray that lets us experience His life in us and releases that life to trickle, sometimes gush, out of us into others.

I call it the PAPA prayer.

part one

Getting Ready to Pray
THE PAPA PRAYER

chapter one

&

YOUR DREAM OF THE PERFECT PAPA
CAN COME TRUE

*I*n my sixty years of living, I have preached, I suppose, a thousand sermons. I've delivered at least that many classroom lectures, and I can't begin to guess how many conference and seminar workshop talks I've given.

But if my aging memory still serves me well, in all those venues, my main topic has never been prayer. I have spoken of it, if at all, only in passing, and a rather quick pass at that.

I haven't bothered to make an accurate count, but I think I have written twenty books. Several dozen journal articles have my byline and probably ten thousand letters my signature. In none of these have I made a serious attempt to discuss prayer. One reason, I think, is that any discussion of prayer, when offered in print or from behind a podium, tends to be heard as instruction more than discussion. For good cause, no band of disciples has yet turned to me and said, "Teach us to pray."

I write this book on prayer as a self-confessed and ecstatic first grader in God's school who is just now learning the alphabet. I write with the excitement of a child when he discovers that his arrangement of letters actually spells a word. I leave it to those far more advanced than I to bring words together into sentences.

At this point (I hope it will be different in ten years), my best thoughts on prayer can be expressed in four letters that fall together to form the word *PAPA*.

WE ALL WANT A PAPA

A little background on what that word means to me will let you know why I like it so much. My father always called his father *Papa*. He lost his papa when he was five years old. When he would tell me what he remembered of his papa in the five years he knew him, Dad's eyes would turn away from me, and he would speak as one happily lost in a better world. It was the same look that came over him when he prayed. I didn't understand that look until recently.

Dad's favorite story—there were many—compared his papa to his best friend Jimmy's father. Every night when he heard his father walk up the stairs to the second-floor apartment next to where my dad lived, Jimmy knew what was coming. If he made one false move, he got the belt from a drunken father.

My dad often told me how bad he felt for Jimmy. Especially because Dad's story was so different. The sound of his papa's footsteps meant the arrival of his hero, a man of towering strength who bent low to care for his children, a gentle giant.

He told me, "Papa always went to Mother and kissed her first, then he turned to each of us kids and hugged us. And then he sat down, sometimes on the floor, and talked to us. I felt safe. Papa was there. What could go wrong? I always wondered why God allowed my papa to die and the monster in Jimmy's home to live."

I never remember Dad referring to his father as *Father* or *Dad* or *Daddy*. It was always *Papa*.

At first, that embarrassed me. It seemed undignified, too sentimental. The term closed a gap between two persons that I was more comfortable leaving open. A little distance left me feeling more myself, more independent and in control. One of my great regrets that I shall carry to my grave is never getting past that proud silliness and drawing as close to my father, my papa, as I secretly wished I could.

I suspect something similar is true for you. I haven't met many sons or daughters who were (or are) as close to their fathers as they wanted to be. Given what I know of families, your father was probably not the sort of person you would call *Papa*. He wasn't (or isn't) a man you longed to draw close to. But you can't stop wishing he were.

Or maybe like me, you were one of the fortunate few. Like mine, your dad deeply loved God. God held first place in his heart, which meant that he could love you all the better. And perhaps there were depths in your father's hidden being that you longed to enter. But you never did, either because he was too private to let you in or you were too scared to make the effort. Both were true for me.

Whatever your background, you and I have this in common: we all wanted, and still want, a papa. We dream of the perfect papa. We yearn for a strong man we can count on to be there for us, to want us, to look after us, to delight in us; someone we want to get close to, a lion of a man who invites us to draw near to him and rest in his powerful but gentle love.

Well, we have one. His name is God. And like the best Papa we can imagine, the sound of His footsteps, if we know who's coming, inspires exuberant joy, not cowering fear. And when we hear His voice and feel His hug, all is well. We're safe. Papa is here. What can go wrong?

EMBRACING OUR HEAVENLY PAPA

But for many Christians, something's not right. We can't hear the sound of His footsteps as He enters our lives. Or if we do, we back away. We might even cringe. Just hearing the word *Papa* or *Daddy* or *Father* provokes feelings of pain or absence in many of us.

When we do sense His warm, strong presence, we have a hard time saying, "Papa is here." It's easier to say "God" than "Papa." The idea that our heavenly Father is sitting on the floor, holding out His arms to embrace us when we run to Him, seems far-fetched, impossible, unthinkable. We have no reference point—it never happened with our earthly dad. We've never known the papa of our dreams.

By now, you may be realizing that this book is really a personal narrative presented as a discussion on prayer. It's the story of my recent discovery of four letters that spell PAPA. (I hope you can see why that word means something special to me.) It's my story of realizing that the gap between my heavenly Papa and me is forever closed and of my growing comfort with a level of intimacy I've never known with my earthly dad and have therefore feared was unavailable.

I hope when you finish this book, the word *Papa* will draw you and not push you away. I hope every dream you've ever dreamed of having a perfect father will seem within reach. Because it is.

If your prayer life has been like mine—dull, intense only during crisis, more requesting than relational, frequently confusing and lacking in confidence, occasionally meaningful and passionate but more often lifelessly routine—join me in the first-grade classroom as together we inexpertly and clumsily try to get the right letters in sequence to spell PAPA. It's surprisingly fun. And it will carry you into the world of heavenly reality—where our best dreams come true.

chapter two

∞

Introducing the PAPA Prayer

*E*ver since I've been a Christian, I've asked God for lots of things He hasn't given. There have been times I've begged God for clear guidance on how to handle messy relationships or on what direction to move in a confusing situation, and it never came. I could name a dozen nasty spots in my life, probably more, when I've felt desperate to hear from God yet heard only silence.

Sometimes I tried to believe I had heard God's voice, but I knew I really hadn't. I wanted it so badly I pretended I had.

"God, where are You?" I've often asked. "Are You listening to me? Do You know what's going on in my life? Do You care? Do I even know who You are?"

In my fifty-two years as a Christian, I haven't yet known God in the same way I've known people I could see and touch and audibly hear. I know my wife, Rachael, in ways I don't know the Father, and I mean personal ways, not physical ones. I know Kep and Ken, my sons, in ways I don't know God's Son. And I know special friends like Trip, Jim, Evan, Glen, and Kent in ways I don't know God's Spirit. Yet the Spirit is inside me, nearer than human friends could ever be.

But all that's changing. Not completely, of course. Complete change comes when we get home. But enough change is going on to give me fresh hope that more is ahead in this life. Something good is happening inside me that's new, after all these years of being a Christian. Perhaps what encourages me most is that this new hope grows stronger on bad days, and I still have plenty of those.

Knowing my real Papa is meaning more to me. I can now report that there are moments of encounter with God that are more real and reach deeper and produce more joy than my best encounters with others, including my wife, my kids, and my closest friends.

Emptiness, loneliness, thirst, and hunger still plague me, along with irritability, discouragement, and boredom. I still have dark days. But now these experiences sometimes seem more like open doorways into a better world than thick walls trapping me in this one.

Now when I ask God for things I want, I'm more aware that He's listening. And I feel less demanding, less as if I'm trying to control God, to get Him to do certain things that, rightly or wrongly, matter to me. Every once in a while, I'm staggered by the thought that He's having a great time doing me good right now, no matter what's happening. He wants me to be as happy as He can make me. And I'm realizing for that to happen, I must give up on the happiness I can find elsewhere. That doesn't mean I'm not to enjoy a good meal or good friendship; it means I'm not to depend on or require the good things of life for my well-being, or to figure out how I can get God to give me the legitimate blessings of life that I want—or when I get them, to ask them to fill me up more then they can.

The best change is that now I'm hearing from God in a way I haven't before. Sometimes, though never audibly, I hear the Father speak more clearly than I hear the voice of a human friend. In an increasing number of situations—some seemingly trivial, like whether to get up when I wake up before the alarm goes off, and some of more obvious consequence, like what to say to my wife in an argument or what topic to select for a talk

I'm scheduled to give the next morning—in situations like these, I sometimes know exactly what to do. I know as surely as I know it would be a good thing to remember my wedding anniversary.

All these changes are directly the work of God. But He's working through a vehicle He's given me. That vehicle is a new understanding of prayer that, although still shallow and perhaps new only to me, is far deeper and richer—and simpler—than anything I've known before.

A NEW WAY OF PRAYING

I've practiced centering prayer. I've contemplatively prayed. I've prayed liturgically. I've interceded and petitioned. The first model of prayer I learned as a kid was ACTS: adoration, confession, thanksgiving, supplication. I tried that, too, for years. I've benefited from each, and I still do. In ways you'll see, elements of each style are still with me. There are many good ways to pray.

But I believe I've sovereignly stumbled on a fresh way to think about prayer that has led me to a new way of praying. It's not a formula or technique. There are no techniques in good conversation with God. There are no means to manipulate Him, no ways to persuade Him to do things our way. He's not open to input on how best to run my life.

What I want to share with you is rather a way to relate to God that lets us hear Him speak. It's not just a way to wait for Him or to listen to Him or to focus on Him. All those are included, but what I want to share with you is a way of coming to God that delights Him and changes us. It's a way to pray that brings us into union with Him, so that it is no longer we who live but Christ who lives through us. It's a way to know God so well that the deepest desire of His heart actually becomes the deepest desire of ours, and that frees us to ask God for what we really want with confidence that He'll move heaven and earth to grant our requests, because what we want now matches what He wants.

It's the PAPA prayer, and it looks like this:

P: *Present yourself to God without pretense.* Be a real person in the relationship. Tell Him whatever is going on inside you that you can identify.

A: *Attend to how you're thinking of God.* Again, no pretending. Ask yourself, "How am I experiencing God right now?" Is He a vending machine, a frowning father, a distant, cold force? Or is He your gloriously strong but intimate Papa?

P: *Purge yourself of anything blocking your relationship with God.* Put into words whatever makes you uncomfortable or embarrassed when you're real in your relationship with Him. How are you thinking more about yourself and your satisfaction than about anyone else, including God and His pleasure?

A: *Approach God as the "first thing" in your life,* as your most valuable treasure, the Person you most want to know. Admit that other people and things really do matter more to you right now, but you long to want God so much that every other good thing in your life becomes a "second-thing" desire.

That's what I call relational prayer. And I'm coming to see that it belongs in the exact center of my prayer life—for that matter, in the center of my entire spiritual journey. Nothing has relieved my confusion over unanswered prayer requests more than the realization that relational prayer must always come before petitionary prayer. Relate and then request. Enjoy God and then enjoy His provisions, whatever they are.

Power in petition of God depends on depth of relationship with God. The PAPA prayer is the best way I've discovered to develop and nourish the relationship with God given to me by Jesus through His life, death, and resurrection. Relational prayer provides the Spirit with a wide open opportunity to do what He loves most to do, to draw me into the heart and life of the Father and to make me more like the Son.

Usually, when I pray the PAPA prayer, nothing happens—at least nothing I can see or feel right away. Sometimes I feel closer to God, or at least I think I do. And sometimes I sense an urge to do something, to reflect on a certain thought, to call a certain person, to think about a certain passage in the Bible, or to read a certain book.

More often, I feel and hear nothing. Praying the PAPA prayer is not rubbing a magic lantern and making known three requests to a docile genie that pops out before our eyes. It's simply a way to come to God and learn to wait, to listen with a little less wax in our spiritual ears, and, most of all, to be relentlessly real.

RELATIONAL PRAYER LEADS TO PERSONAL TRANSFORMATION

Here's what I'm realizing: coming to God in this way creates space in me that the Spirit always fills. Always. I may not know it's happening, but it is. Like nature, the Spirit always fills a vacuum. But we're so busy filling our emptiness, there's not much of a vacuum for Him to fill. That's why narcissists never meet God. They're too busy trying to fill themselves.

As I pray the PAPA prayer, over time I begin to see that my attitude is different. I see my sin more quickly and clearly than I see someone else's, even in an argument. I find myself relating differently with God and with others. I feel a little less of that damnable spirit of entitlement. I'm a little less whiny and demanding, a little less superior and condescending.

And I realize I'm a little less into myself, which lets me love better.

I notice that I ask God for different kinds of things and with a different attitude. I still plead for more energy, but without the same spirit of complaint; and I plead even more for a perspective on my fatigue that lets me know God is up to something good even when I stay tired, that He's always doing me good and enjoying Himself in the process.

As I recognize the symptoms of advancing years and terrifying images of old age come to mind, I am developing a comforting sense that the best is yet to come, even if I end up alone in a nursing home with attendants taking care of me.

And God, my real Papa, is becoming more real. I can see that I'm on my way to wanting Him more than any other blessing I can imagine. And sometimes, not often, I hear His voice. I'm becoming part of the divine conversation. I'm becoming a participant in the divine nature. And that's union with God.

Through the path opened by Jesus and by the power of the Spirit in God's Word, I'm coming to know my Papa. And that's forming the life of Jesus in me. I want to please God and reveal Him to others at any cost, more than I want any other blessing. And that's just like Jesus.

The PAPA prayer is simply a way to open dialogue with God, to relate with Him more intimately and honestly than I relate with anyone else. It helps me become more interested in listening than speaking, more eager to hear His voice than for Him to hear mine. It's a way of cleaning out my ears so I can become an attentive and discerning listener to God.

It's also a way to make room in my soul that He loves to fill, to clean out the rubbish I pile into my inner world so that He can fill me with His reality. It helps me realize that to experience God, I must experience Him in the way I relate to others, that I must behave toward others with the divine energy and wisdom He's already put in me.

And it's a way of surrendering my tongue, that hardest of all beasts to tame (James 3:7–8). It brings together what I most want and what the Father most wants to give. It lets me ask for first things, for what really matters in life, with more eagerness than I ask for second things. I'm coming to see that my health, my family's health, my marriage, my ministry, my bank account, even whether my children are walking with God, are all second things in comparison to the first thing of knowing God, of enjoying Him and trusting Him and serving Him and becoming more like Him.

The PAPA prayer puts relating with God ahead of asking things from God. It stirs me to value knowing Him more than getting something from Him. And the better I get to know Him, the more I know I'm in for everything my heart could desire, because He loves to make me happy. When I put first things first, I become more confident that second things are on their way. With delight, I realize that God is running our relationship. It gives Him the first word in our conversation, and the last.

Relational Prayer Lets Us Hear God's Voice

If there were no other advantages, the fact that the PAPA prayer lets me hear His voice would be enough. I heard Him just yesterday. I was reading Jeremiah 32:40–41, in which God says this to the people alive then and to those who would live after Jesus's death and resurrection: "I will never stop doing good to them. . . . I will rejoice in doing them good . . . with all my heart and soul."

The Spirit carried those words to my heart. I was overwhelmed with joy. All I could think of was how badly I wanted to make that good news known to others by the way I treated them. A friend who has been driving me crazy came to mind. I wanted to call him, not to point out how he's been annoying me but to do him good. I made that call, and I was humbled and broken by my superior attitude that all of a sudden seemed silly and beneath me.

Let me tell you this: once you hear from God, you're hooked. You love your own voice less, and that feels like freedom. You realize you'll never hear a sweeter voice than His, at once infinitely strong and infinitely gentle, the blended voice of the Lion and the Lamb. Listening for that voice becomes what you most want to do. The PAPA prayer is one way to become a listener and to hear what God is saying, and in the process to experience Christ's life coming out of you.

But why am I seeing this only now, after all these years? I want to talk about that before I get into the specifics of the PAPA prayer.

chapter three

🙢

Prayer Used to Be Dull, but Not Now

*I*ve been praying for a long time. Why is it different now? I think you'll better understand the PAPA prayer, what makes it unique, and why I'm excited about it if you understand a little of my journey from lifeless words to dialogue with God.

When I was growing up, prayer meetings were the dullest part of my church experience. The annual Sunday school picnic was the most exciting. We played softball, ate hot dogs, and spit watermelon seeds, and the only prayer was a short one thanking God for the food.

Sermons I could endure because at least someone had his eyes open and was talking to people I could see. And the singing for ten minutes before the sermon was fun. I liked to sing tenor and throw Mother—who could barely carry a tune—off key.

But prayer meetings were boring. And senseless. I just didn't get the point. I suspect that says more about my immaturity than about the meetings themselves. Dad seemed to really enjoy them. I could never figure that out. We'd all close our eyes and tell someone I'd never met named God how wonderful He was for sending Jesus to the cross and giving us the Bible, and then we'd ask Him for all sorts of things we wanted.

As near as I could tell, these things either happened or didn't happen whether we prayed about them or not. Sometimes I'd hear someone say, "We need to get this request on the prayer chain." At first I wasn't sure if that was our Protestant version of rosary beads, but when I found out that it meant asking more people to pray, I wondered why fifty prayers for the same thing had more clout with God than two or three, or even just one.

When something happened that we prayed for, we'd all smile at each other and say thank you to God. I once overheard a man say, "Well, of course Sarah got better. We prayed about it." When Sarah got worse a few months later, we all prayed again. She didn't get better the second go-round. I don't recall anyone wondering out loud what went wrong. Unanswered prayer never got much mention.

When I thought about it, I was confused. So I didn't think about it much. All I knew about prayer was to ask for things in case God might give them to me and to thank Him when He did. I grew up loosely committed to the "just-in-case" prayers. You know the kind—pray for something just in case it makes a difference. I don't know how God put up with my immaturity. Maybe He liked the fact that at least I was talking to Him. I'd say a just-in-case prayer the morning of a big test. I did it again when I put twelve applications to graduate school in the mailbox and again when Dad went in for surgery.

I saved my "tell-God-how-wonderful-He-is" prayers for when good things happened, like when Dad returned home all better. I could muster up a little sincerity then.

A PRAYER FACE-LIFT, INSTEAD OF A TRANSPLANT

That pattern continued into adulthood, with two modifications. First, telling God how wonderful He was became part of what my church called worship. This kind of prayer shifted away from praying for things into an expression of my desire to enjoy His wonderfulness, and I expressed that desire most often in music. I must have sung "As the Deer" and "Open the Eyes of My Heart" more than a thousand times. I still sing those choruses. I like them. And I think God still likes it when I sing them.

But articulating my longings through that kind of music became for me the extent of worship. For most of my adult life, the notion that worship at its core is sacrifice never took hold. I'm not sure I ever heard it. I went along with my church culture, which seemed to think worship was about feeling emotional about God, especially when He behaved properly, which meant that He did what we asked Him to do. Then we shared our appreciation in musical and sentence prayers when we felt better. Prayer was all about us. Even our worship seemed narcissistic. I don't think it was that way for Dad. But it was for me. And I suspect for a few others.

The second modification was really a kind of face-lift. As a kid, my just-in-case prayers were pretty routine, a passionless recitation of a daily liturgy of requests. Unless, of course, something big was at stake, like Dad going in for surgery. Then I became zealous.

Looking back, I think my occasional fervency was a mixture of panic and demand: I was terrified about something, and I really thought God should help out. But as time went on, my fervent prayers became a little more humble and, I think, more trusting. I knew demanding was out of line when I talked to God, and I was more convinced that God had some good purpose in whatever happened, even though I knew I might have to wait until heaven to see what was good about arthritis and cancer.

So for years, my tell-God-how-wonderful-He-is prayers became an expression through music of my deep longing to experience God, and I called it worship. And my just-in-case prayers lost some of their energy of entitlement and gained some of the humility and trust appropriate to those who petition God. Those were good changes, but they were only a face-lift when a transplant was needed.

THE PAPA PRAYER—A LIFELINE TO GOD

It's only been in recent years—and I'm now entering my seventh decade—that prayer has become the richest part of my spiritual life. It's my lifeline. Without prayer—a radically different kind of prayer than the two I've mentioned—panic would still be running my life, and I'd still be religiously demanding all sorts of things to keep me stable and happy.

Without the PAPA prayer, God would still be a three-letter word I would be trying to believe meant something, rather than the three-person community I'm learning to relate with and enjoy. Without prayer, the new kind, I suppose I'd still be writing and teaching and counseling, but it would mostly be a lot of activity with only a little power and even less satisfaction and meaning.

But with the kind of prayer I want to tell you about in this book, I'm now sensing what I believe is the rhythm of the Father's Spirit moving me as I write and teach and counsel. I don't move all that well with the rhythm sometimes, and too often I still don't feel it, but there is a difference. At times I actually experience more joy in loving others than in being loved, because I'm believing more deeply in my heart and not just in my head that I'm already loved by God and that His love is moving me.

With the PAPA prayer, I'm aware that I'm responding to the Father's love by falling in love with Him. On good days, I believe that He really enjoys my company. He likes having me around. With prayer, a kind I never prayed as a kid or even until recently, I'm experiencing true freedom—the freedom to be a lover of God and a lover of people. That, I'm realizing, is what Jesus set me free for.

I don't always love terribly well. Some days and with some people, you'd have a right to wonder if I even know God, if I bear any family resemblance to my Father, if I'm an adopted but still undisciplined child. There's a battle going on inside me that I sometimes lose. But with prayer, I'm more able to be honest about where I fail and accept proper guilt without hating myself; I'm more able to like the fact that I can't manage God, that I can't make Him show up when I want and how I want; I'm more able to be broken over my hidden failures that you can't see rather than just the ones I'm forced to admit; and I'm more able to regard everything I want in this life as a huge bunch of second things compared to the first thing of knowing God and becoming a little Christ.

When I say that prayer is now my lifeline, I'm not talking about prayer as I used to understand it. Before, I thought prayer was all about trying to coax God into giving me something and then thanking Him on those rare occasions when I was successful. Now I see that prayer has more to do with God's speaking to me and my learning to be the listener. It's a dance where He leads.

I'm starting to hear, to really hear, the voice of God. And I'm realizing He likes me. He loves me and He speaks to me. He likes it when I show up for the party He's throwing. Somewhere deep inside me, I sometimes hear music from another world, and the rhythm releases what is good and alive in me into others. And that's a kick. It's a party. I know it sounds a little bit crazy, but sometimes I picture myself dancing, first with God and then into other people's lives. Sometimes it's more than a picture. Sometimes it's real. And that's a real kick.

For the first time in my life, I like to pray. I don't find it boring. And it's because I'm now seeing that relational prayer, praying to know God and to enjoy being known by Him, supplies the right kind of passion for petitionary and thanksgiving prayers, for asking God to give me what I desire and for thanking Him for every blessing I receive.

chapter four

❧

Get God Before Praying to Get Things from God

$\mathcal{O}$f all the ways the Bible invites us to pray, petitionary prayer—asking God for the things we want—is perhaps the most practiced and the most bewildering. And it's also the most abused. I write about it in this chapter with one purpose in mind: to restore petitionary prayer to its privileged and powerful place in the lives of God's children, which is after relational prayer and after a few other kinds of prayer as well.

The Bible indicates at least five distinct ways that we can communicate with God through prayer. We can relate with Him, worship Him, thank Him for who He is and what He does for us, intercede for others in response to their needs, and petition Him for blessings we'd like Him to provide.

THE PROCESS OF COMMUNICATING WITH GOD IN PRAYER

First, we start with *relational prayer*. This is what Jesus had in mind when He told us to remain in Him, to abide in Him as a branch sticks close to the vine (John 15:4–7). The PAPA prayer is one form of relational prayer that, in my view, has the potential to bring us more fully into contact with

God than other forms. Other forms of relating to God that have unique value in connecting us to Him include contemplative prayer and centering prayer.

Second, when we're caught up with who it is we're relating to, *prayers of worship and adoration* naturally follow. We fall to our knees in amazement when it dawns on us that the God of creation, the sovereign ruler and Lord of the universe, is our Papa. His might awes us. But His grace reduces us to head-shaking silence. We can get close to Him, like a child with her daddy. It's mind-boggling. He's just too good for words, unlike anyone we've ever met.

Our relationship with and worship of God lead us to *prayers of thanksgiving*, for Him and for all His blessings. It should be noted that only when we're first overwhelmed with who God is can we be properly thankful for what He provides. Skip over prayers of relating and worship, and a hint of shallow, silly entitlement slips into our gratitude.

A friend recently told me that his new car arrived at the dealer two weeks ahead of the scheduled delivery date. "I hadn't traded in my old car in order to make more money on a private sale. It sold the same day the dealer called to tell me the new one arrived early. And I got my asking price. Isn't that something? God is so good. I was really thankful." When convenient things like that happen to me, I can sometimes detect an attitude beneath my appropriate gratitude that says, "That's how things should happen. God's doing His job. He's keeping His promise to make my life go well."

Efforts to worship God without first getting to know Him tend to reduce worship to mere appreciation when God cooperates with our agendas. And thanking God without true worship, without first being stunned that the holy God who has every right to abandon us instead draws us closer, leaves us still thinking that at least a few things ought to go our way. But when true worship is the spring from which gratitude flows, we take nothing for granted. The fact that anything is right in our lives becomes a cause for celebration, and we feel humble gratitude for undeserved blessings—which, of course, all of them are.

As we get to know God, worship Him, and thank Him in all things, our hearts go out to others, including rejecting spouses, irritating teenagers, and betraying friends. The mind of Christ takes over, and we become more concerned for others than for ourselves. We care more about their relationship with God than their impact on us. We want them to know God, worship Him, and live lives of gratitude to Him as we do. So we naturally turn to *prayers of intercession.* We pray on their behalf with selfless motives.

But if we intercede for others without attending to our own relationship with God, our intercession will have more to do with our well-being than with theirs. "God, change my spouse so I won't hurt so much." "Soften my child's heart so I won't be so worried." "Change so-and-so in my small group so I'll enjoy my involvement more." Intercession that does not flow out of knowing God ourselves, worshiping Him for who He is, and humbly thanking Him for whatever He provides will be indelibly stained with self-centeredness. And we may not even recognize it. We are, after all, praying for good things to happen in the lives of others. What exactly is wrong with that? It's hard to see that we might be thinking more of ourselves than them.

But when relational prayer yields worship and worship produces gratitude and gratitude leads us to intercede for others to know God as we've come to know Him, then we intercede "in the Spirit" with other-centered love.

And that process sets the stage for *prayers of petition* to flow out of a surrendered heart. "God, may my surgery go well, may I make more money, may I feel more energy, may I find more friends, but grant me these personal comforts only if they will not interfere with but will rather enhance the formation of Christ in me." When I want to be like Jesus more than I want anything else, then I pray, "Not my will but Thine be done. Above all else, may Your kingdom come."

GETTING THE PRIORITIES OF PRAYER MIXED UP

Suppose you start with petitionary prayer and give no real time or focus to knowing God more richly, worshiping Him more deeply, thanking Him more humbly, or interceding for others more selflessly. Don't relate to God; use Him instead. Worship Him for the visible good He does you, not for the supreme worth of His being. Disguise your spirit of entitlement in the cloak of thanksgiving, expressing gratitude for what you really think God should give you anyway. Intercede for others with your happiness and comfort in view.

Then go to God in petitionary prayer. Ask Him for whatever you want. In that condition of heart, your prayers will have as much influence on God as the whinings of a two-year-old on good parents.

I don't want to discourage you from asking God for what you desire. But I do want you to first delight yourself in the Lord, to love Him with all your being, and to then ask boldly for whatever desires arise out of your God-obsessed heart. If your relationship with God is not the growing foundation for asking things of God, then petitionary prayer will become hopelessly bewildering and frustrating.

If you try to get things from God without first praying to get more of God Himself, your petitions will sound more like the rantings of a spoiled brat than the requests of a dependent child. We'll look at the confusing corruption of petitionary prayer in the next chapter and suggest how to restore requests to their privileged and wonderful place in the lives of God's children.

chapter five

The Prayer of a Spoiled Child

$\mathcal{J}$esus said, "You may ask me for anything in my name, and I will do it" (John 14:14). Anything? Well, that's what He said.

Then Jesus said it again, this time with stronger emphasis and an added guarantee of joy: "I tell you the truth [He leaves no room for quibbling; He wants us to know He means what He says], my Father will give you whatever you ask in my name." Anything! Whatever! "Ask and you will receive, and your joy will be complete" (John 16:23–24). Petitionary prayer is a good thing. Jesus told us to ask Him for whatever we want.

"ASK AND YOU WILL RECEIVE" . . . ANYTHING?

I was eight years old, and I had just watched another episode of *Superman* on TV. I could think of nothing I wanted more than to fly. Desire consumed me. Last week's Sunday school lesson came to mind: "Ask and you will receive."

I went outside. Standing on our driveway, I bowed my head and prayed, "God, let me fly like Superman." I jumped as high as I could (maybe eight inches), claiming God's promise. A half-second later, I landed with a thud on the concrete.

These verses embarrass us. We can't get them to work. Then we notice an out. Jesus narrowed things with the qualifying phrase "in my name." The dozen explanations I've heard of what Jesus meant boil down to this: He promises to give us anything we ask for that suits His purposes. And since He's sovereign and a lot smarter than we are, we're told that's a good thing. But it leaves me wondering why we should bother to pray if He's going to do what He knows is best anyway. Just sit in the back of the bus and leave the driving to Him. That's one metaphor. Here's another.

Prayer can sometimes seem more like feeding money into a slot machine than making requests of a loving Father. Jackpot stories get written up. Those who walk away with empty pockets—well, they just walk away and try to hang on to their faith in prayer as best they can.

Like my friend. He recently woke up at two in the morning wracked with pain over his two adult children. One won't talk to him. The other is openly gay and hurt that his parents don't accept his "alternative" lifestyle.

For more than an hour, my friend prayed, he sobbed, he begged. "God, work in Maria's life. I'm not even asking that she speak to me. I just want her to know You and to feel some hope in her life. And Brent—oh God! I can't accept what You reject. But I know You don't reject him. You love him. And I do too. Please let him realize that what he really wants is Your love and that he has it. Please, God, please!"

Ever wonder if God is listening? My friend has been praying that same prayer for three years. He can't believe that what he's asking for is not "in Jesus's name." His pastor reverted to the stock truism that God always answers every prayer with yes, no, or wait.

But that's not a fair reading of Jesus's words. It requires real maneuvering to make Him mean something other than, "Ask for anything, and if it fits My heart and character, I'll say yes every time." How many saints have prayed prayers that seemed a shoo-in to meet that standard but remained unanswered? If God's heart is love and His character is good, then prayer for someone's salvation has to fit. Doesn't it?

My grandmother prayed till she died at ninety that her older son, Dad's brother, would declare faith in Jesus. She waited a long time, and she died with that unanswered prayer still on her lips. A couple of decades later, my uncle passed on to the next world without, to my knowledge, ever turning to Christ for salvation. What on earth do all the prayer promises mean?

My friend, the father of the estranged daughter and gay son, called yesterday. "I've been reading and rereading the parable of the persistent widow. I just don't get it."

This parable is written in Luke's Gospel. It goes like this:

> Then Jesus told his disciples a parable to show them that they should always pray and not give up. He said: "In a certain town there was a judge who neither feared God nor cared about men. And there was a widow in that town who kept coming to him with the plea, 'Grant me justice against my adversary.'
>
> "For some time he refused. But finally he said to himself, 'Even though I don't fear God or care about men, yet because this widow keeps bothering me, I will see that she gets justice, so that she won't eventually wear me out with her coming!'"
>
> And the Lord said, "Listen to what the unjust judge says. And will not God bring about justice for his chosen ones, who cry out to him day and night? Will he keep putting them off? I tell you, he will see that they get justice, and quickly. However, when the Son of Man comes, will he find faith on the earth?" (Luke 18:1–8)

It's hard to miss the point. It's even harder to spin it to fit our experience. Jesus was pretty clear: keep praying, don't quit; and if you stay with it, your request will be granted, sooner rather than later.

But that's not what's happening. Sincere people all over the world cry out to God and get no answer. A friend just died of Lou Gehrig's disease despite the intense prayers of many. Fill a room with a thousand honest Christians; ask them to stand up if they've been asking God for something unselfish and good for a long time that has not yet been given, and nine hundred will get to their feet.

Why? Is God listening or not? Does praying make any real difference in what happens? We've all heard by now that prayed-for hospital patients have fewer medical complications and better recovery rates than unprayed-for patients. Has that been your experience? Has your child's asthma continued despite your faithful and fervent prayer? Does your friend still get disabling migraines? Are we supposed to keep on asking for things we never seem to get? What's the point?

How about prayers for wisdom? Are any of you right now facing a tricky situation that you're not sure how to handle? Perhaps a tension with your spouse? How should you talk to your husband when all love is gone? Or how do you decide whether to change churches or to switch jobs, or maybe where to look for a new church or job?

What do you do with the verse that tells us to ask God for wisdom but only with absolute confidence that it will be given? The person who requests God's wisdom for knowing what to do when life gets rough needs to pray without doubting. That's what James says (1:6). The one who, for whatever reason, isn't certain God will answer "should not think he will receive anything from the Lord; he is a double-minded man, unstable in all he does" (vv. 7–8).

Margaret e-mailed me last week. "My son married a drug user who sleeps around. He wants to have us over for dinner because his wife thinks we don't like her. We don't! She's breaking our son's heart, and she has some kind of hold on him. He seems so weak. Do I tell him that? Do we go there for dinner? What should we do?"

Should I write her back and say, "Well, if you want to know what God thinks you should do, you must first have complete confidence He'll tell you if you ask"? Am I hearing James right?

In another place, Christ told us that if our faith was no bigger than a tiny mustard seed, we could tell a mountain to shift location and it would (Matthew 17:20). I've got a few mountains in my life I'd like to move. I'll bet you do too. How do we inflate our faith to a size that will get our prayers to work? Wasn't Jesus's point that even a tiny amount of real faith is enough? Don't many of us have at least the bare minimum? Then why are so many mountains in our lives still sitting in the same spot? It isn't that we haven't prayed, and with at least some faith.

THE PROBLEM WITH THE WAY WE PRAY

One more verse, this one direct from Abba, from Father God, our heavenly Papa. Listen to what He once said to some of His kids who weren't doing so well. Since God doesn't change, we can assume the longing heart from which He spoke to them is the same longing heart from which He's speaking to us right now: "How gladly would I treat you like sons and give you a desirable land" (Jeremiah 3:19).

What's stopping Him? Maybe there's a problem with the way we pray. Or maybe it's the way we don't pray. Consider this: we do a lot more asking of God than relating to God.

But even if that's true, is it a problem? Didn't Jesus tell us to come to Him with our requests? Here's a second thought, and it's revolutionary: *maybe petitionary prayer is supposed to come after relational prayer.*

I wonder what would happen if our prayers were more like the response of a child lost in the big city when he finds his dad?

When our younger son Ken was eight, I took him for a weekend of fun to New York City. The first night in our hotel room, he sat up in bed wearing his Superman pajamas and asked, "Dad, we're here for fun, right?" I nodded. He stared at me, opened his eyes wide, and breathlessly asked, "Can we stay up past eight?" I leaned over, met his eyes, and said, "Let's party!" We ordered pizza, watched a movie on television, and he fell asleep at nine thirty, all partied out. It was a night to remember.

The next day, we played hide-and-seek in Central Park. At one point, I hid behind a tree not more than twenty feet from where he was leaning against another tree, eyes closed, counting to ten.

"Ready or not, here I come!" he shouted. I didn't let him find me. I kept circling the thick tree trunk staying just out of his sight. But he was never out of mine.

After a long two minutes, I saw his excited smile suddenly disappear, and a look of sheer terror came over his face. *Where's Dad? Did he disappear? Did some mugger knock him out and drag him away? Did Jesus come back and take my dad and leave me behind?* I could see these questions in my son's panicked eyes.

I immediately stepped out from behind the tree. "Dad!" he shrieked, and he ran to me. "I was scared I wouldn't find you."

At that moment, he had no thought of the toy-shopping trip I had promised. All he wanted was to be with me, to stay close by my side, to keep me in sight, to go wherever I wanted to go.

Missionary and evangelist E. Stanley Jones wrote, "The first thing in prayer is to get God. If you get Him, everything else follows. Allow God to get at you, to invade you, to take possession of you. He then pours His very prayers through you. They are His prayers—God-inspired, and hence, God answered.

"Prayer's like the fastening of the cup to the wounded side of a pine tree to allow the resin to pour into it. You are now nestling up into the side of God—the wounded side, if you will—and you allow His grace to fill you up. You are taking in the very life of God."[1]

Christian writer Ravi Zacharias put it this way: "Prayer is not the means of bringing our will to pass but the means by which He brings our will into line to gladly receive His will." And then Ravi adds this counsel: "Find a plan for your times of prayer and implement it to His honor and glory and for your joy and sustenance."[2]

The great need of people in the church today, and perhaps in your life, is to better relate to God. And the best way for all of us to do that is to find a plan for our time of prayer that draws us near to God for the sheer joy of encounter before we ask Him for a thing. Relational prayer must become the platform and context for petitionary prayer. We'll never understand petitionary prayer until we learn to practice relational prayer, until we nestle up into the wounded side of God and let Him pour His life into our empty cup. Even then it will still be a mystery, but a delightful mystery, not an annoying one.

The PAPA Prayer—A Way to Relate with God

More than anything else, the PAPA prayer is a relational prayer. It's the foundation for understanding a little better and for powerfully practicing petitionary prayer. It's a prayer that girls and boys can pray to their daddy. Unless we become as little children who approach our heavenly Papa just to be near Him, something in our hearts will keep us confused and frustrated when we ask God for what we want. Worse, we'll be haughty and demanding. And worse yet, we may not see how haughty and demanding we are.

After fifty years of being a Christian, and a pretty sincere one most of that time, the PAPA prayer is doing something deep inside me that's not been done before. It's opening my eyes to see not only a new way to live but also a new way to pray.

The PAPA prayer brings together everything I've been thinking about since I began the Christian life. It's helping me want to touch God more than wanting to put the touch on God. I offer it to you as a plan for restoring relationship with God to its place at the center of your life, and for reclaiming the privilege of asking for whatever we want in His name. When the Son of Man returns, He'll find the faith He's looking for in the heart of every Christian who has drawn close enough to God to trust Him with everything. The PAPA prayer can help us do that. It can help bring us into life-giving and life-changing union with God.

Fix relational prayer in the exact center of your life. See every day as an opportunity to relate more intimately with your heavenly Papa and to bring His kingdom into your specific circumstances by the way you relate to others. That's what Jesus did, in the power of the Spirit. And He invited us to do the same thing.

As that happens, as Christians across the world put relational prayer in the center of their lives, the church will recover its power. Union with God will become a growing reality. Desire for Him will surpass every other desire. We'll suffer well, we'll be good stewards of blessings, and we'll live to reveal what our Papa is like to a watching world, to our spouses, kids, friends, and colleagues. We'll relate well to God and to others.

RELATIONAL PRAYER IS THE CENTER OF TRUE PRAYER

Keep the point of this chapter clearly in your mind: *Relational prayer is the center of all true prayer. The power of petitionary prayer depends on the centrality of relational prayer.*

That's exactly what Jesus said. Sit with His disciples in the upper room and listen to His words: "If you remain in me and my words remain in you, ask whatever you wish, and it will be given you." As we're wondering what it means to remain in Him, He goes on: "This is to my Father's glory, that you bear much fruit, showing yourselves to be my disciples" (John 15:7–8).

So that's what He's saying. To remain in Him means to live for the single purpose that ruled His life, with the same passion that kept Him on track. He loved His Father, He loved spending time with His Father in prayer, and He wanted nothing more than to let everyone see how wonderful His Father was, even if it cost Him His life. And that life, His life, is now in us. His passion and purpose are in our hearts.

Every request from Jesus that flowed out of that passion and purpose was answered during His life on earth. And it will be in ours. If we share Christ's passion for His Father and dedicate ourselves at any cost to the purpose of bringing heaven's kingdom to earth by revealing the Father's character in all our relationships, then our petitions will reflect the mind of Christ—and they will be answered.

I reread that last paragraph, and I hear myself saying, "Sounds great. But maybe it's just a bunch of sweet, religious words. I mean, really feeling what Christ feels and wanting what Christ wants when my kid's driving me crazy? Get real! That's out of my reach." If you're saying the same thing, maybe we both need to get serious about relational prayer.

When relational prayer is in the center, it not only shapes our petitions but also changes how we engage in every other kind of prayer. Only on the ground of relationship with God, restored through redemption and nourished through relational prayer, can we properly worship, unselfishly thank God for blessings, intercede for others, and ask things for ourselves.

Remove relational prayer from the center, and every other kind of prayer goes bad. Worship becomes blasphemy—we reduce God to our errand boy; He's there to serve us. Thanksgiving becomes a disguised expression of entitlement—we thank God for what we think He really should have given us anyway. Intercession is rooted in self-interest—we plead with God on behalf of family, friends, government, and church leaders with our purposes and comfort in mind. And petitions, even apparently legitimate ones such as a loved one's salvation or a child's health, are fueled by the energy of a demanding spirit. We hear ourselves presenting reasonable requests to God. He hears us whining like spoiled kids, "Gimme! Gimme! Gimme!" We have no controlling thought of advancing God's kingdom or of enjoying our privileged relationship with the King. Self-interest rules again.

Take a few minutes and think what prayer looks like in the life of a Christian whose central interest in prayer is petition:

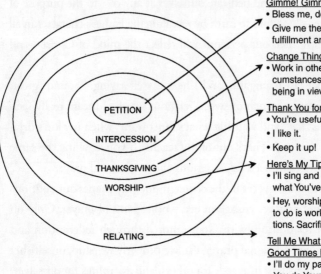

FALSE PRAYER
A Me-Centered Prayer Life

PETITION

INTERCESSION

THANKSGIVING

WORSHIP

RELATING

<u>Gimme! Gimme! Gimme!</u>
• Bless me, dear God.
• Give me the good life of
  fulfillment and joy.

<u>Change Things for My Sake</u>
• Work in others and in my circumstances with my well-
  being in view.

<u>Thank You for My Blessings</u>
• You're useful.
• I like it.
• Keep it up!

<u>Here's My Tip for Good Service</u>
• I'll sing and praise You for
  what You've given me.
• Hey, worship is easy. All I have
  to do is work up fervent emotions. Sacrifice isn't required.

<u>Tell Me What to Do to Keep the
Good Times Rolling</u>
• I'll do my part for as long as
  You do Yours.

Now imagine what your prayer life could be if relational prayer took over the center spot.

TRUE PRAYER
A Relationally-Centered Prayer Life

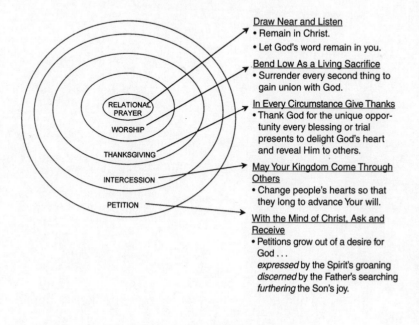

Draw Near and Listen
• Remain in Christ.
• Let God's word remain in you.

Bend Low As a Living Sacrifice
• Surrender every second thing to gain union with God.

In Every Circumstance Give Thanks
• Thank God for the unique opportunity every blessing or trial presents to delight God's heart and reveal Him to others.

May Your Kingdom Come Through Others
• Change people's hearts so that they long to advance Your will.

With the Mind of Christ, Ask and Receive
• Petitions grow out of a desire for God . . .
expressed by the Spirit's groaning
discerned by the Father's searching
furthering the Son's joy.

RELATIONAL PRAYER
WORSHIP
THANKSGIVING
INTERCESSION
PETITION

That's prayer. And it begins with the PAPA prayer.

chapter six

❧

Relational Prayer Is About God and Me

I'm afraid we'll merely play with the PAPA prayer for a day or two and not really pray it as a lifestyle, unless we get rid of the notion that the center of prayer is asking for things.

The true center of prayer, its real point, is relating to God. When we restore relational prayer to its rightful place, then petitionary prayer is restored to its rightful and powerful place as an expression of our love for God, not as the chance to get whatever we want for ourselves.

But we don't naturally think of prayer as an opportunity to relate with God. Most of us find our prayer lives dominated by asking God for things. For most of us, that's what prayer is. Changing our minds about the point of prayer will be tough. The wrong idea is nearly universal and deeply imbedded in our thinking.

But if we hold to it, if we keep on believing that prayer is more about getting things than getting God, not only will we eventually get thoroughly confused when prayer doesn't "work," but talking to God will at some point feel boring as well. If we're honest.

As one friend told me, "Things right now are really bad. A couple of years back, situations like this would drive me to my knees. But now, I have no clue how to pray or why I should even bother. I think I used to pray just to cover my bases. But now I don't have any energy to talk to God."

GETTING PREPARED FOR RELATIONAL PRAYER

I'm starting to think that getting fed up with asking God for what we want is not such a bad thing. It prepares us for relational prayer.

My wife and I have for years prayed the same simple petitionary prayer every morning. She begins, "Help us to recognize and resist the evil one." I finish with, "And draw us closer into Yourself and to each other." It takes about five seconds. We miss only a few days per year.

Those are requests, and they are good. We'll keep asking them till we die. It hasn't gotten old yet. But it could.

For years, our natural tendency when we pray has been to ask, not relate; to offer up monologues, not engage in conversation. But now Rachael and I are recognizing that inclination, and we're actually praying differently.

Just last night we got word that the son of close friends is taking his first step out of a pigpen he's lived in for a long time. Our first impulse was to pray, "God, thanks for answering prayers for this kid, and, please, turn his life around." We care deeply for this family, but neither of us had much energy for that kind of familiar prayer.

We stopped ourselves (we've been talking together about this book for weeks) and decided to try to pray relationally. Rachael told God how hopeful she felt. I told God that I was cautiously excited. That was the beginning of our conversation with God. It was how we *presented* ourselves. It took about five minutes to think about it, discern it, and say it to God.

Then we *attended* to how we pictured God. Who was this God we were talking to? How were we seeing Him, right then? Was He a reluctant judge who would grant our requests if we made them properly? Was He distant and occupied with bigger things? Or was He perhaps a scowling Father who was muttering, "It's about time this rotten kid straightened out"?

As we talked about it, the image surfaced of a father hoisting his robes and running out to welcome the prodigal home. We believed that image came from the Spirit through our familiarity with the Bible. We heard from God. It made us feel a little more eager to continue the conversation. That was our version of attending to God.

Purging came next. Even though we were experiencing God as recklessly eager to reach this prodigal, Rachael told God she felt a little jaded, a little cynical about whether the boy's movement was real. I admitted that I could feel some apprehension and a dose of pride mixed in with my cautious excitement. It looked like I might have the opportunity to be involved with this family. Would I be up to the job? Was I wanting to play hero?

Then, with more humility than when our conversation began, we *approached* God together. "God, something deep inside us really wants You to be first in our lives. We long for the power to abandon ourselves more freely to You as two messy people and, in our brokenness, to see Christ trickle out of us into this family." We didn't ask for that. We simply identified and embraced that desire, and we came to God with it.

Then we listened. We reflected. We talked about what seemed most alive within us. Now we wanted to petition God with requests that arose out of our intimacy with Him, which flowed from the life of the Spirit that our connection with Papa had nourished. We wanted to pray in the Spirit, with the mind of Christ, for the glory of the Father.

Relational prayer released petitionary prayer. Rachael asked God to show Himself strong in the boy's parents, so they wouldn't let their desire for their son's conversion become a first thing in their hearts. I followed up by praying that they would move toward their son without demanding anything from God, that they could celebrate their son's beginning movement without depending on it to continue.

Then we added, "And God, we would really like to see this kid come to Christ. It's hard not to see that as Your will." That petition felt more like a child asking her dad for a second piece of cake. He might give it;

He might not. We weren't sure. But it felt good, and it seemed clean to ask for it.

That was our effort to pray relationally, to make our lives at that moment not about us, and not just about God, but about our relationship with God. We wanted to first relate with God ("remain in me"), and then request of God ("ask what you will").

As we get ready to learn the PAPA prayer (which is coming up in part 2), we must first become convinced that relational prayer is the essence of prayer, that we must first be with God and get to know Him before we ask anything from Him. Let me develop that thought in this chapter and then, in the next two chapters, see if it comes out of my head or from the Bible.

Gimme! Gimme! Gimme!

Praying the PAPA prayer is as easy as riding a bicycle—which, of course, is not so easy for a toddler.

Toddlers ride in strollers. They trust whoever is pushing them to not run into walls, and then they sit back and enjoy the ride. And that's a good thing, for toddlers. Strollers are legitimate transportation for toddlers whose sense of balance has not been developed enough (through countless spills) to keep a two-wheeler upright.

Look around your church next Sunday morning. Talk to the regulars about their prayer life. Reflect on your own. You may come to the same conclusion I've reached: the Western church, especially the evangelical wing, is filled with big kids like me, riding in strollers when we should be riding bikes. And our immaturity shows up most in the way we pray.

An old-time Christian leader named C. J. Vaughan once said, "If I wished to humble anyone, I should question him about his prayers. I know nothing to compare with this topic for its sorrowful self-confessions."[1]

Think about it. Older children still riding in strollers through grocery stores are among the most demanding creatures on the planet. They look past the spinach and apples to the boxes of sugar clumps advertised as cereal. And they demand, "Give me that," with no interest in knowing the one hearing their request and even less interest in trusting that person to choose what's best for them.

Petitioning without relationship—that's what our praying so often amounts to, even though it's well disguised. No matter how piously we couch our requests and no matter how passionately we declare our confidence in the Giver's generosity, we stay in a receiving mode. "Gimme! Gimme! Gimme!" It's all about us.

Our prayers of communion and worship sometimes have more to do with staying on God's good side in order to get more blessings than with building our relationship with Him. The idea of knowing God and being known by Him just doesn't seem that important.

For some, it's irrelevant. Children during a long, hot summer may know the ice cream man's name and may even greet him warmly and enjoy his smile, but the point is the ice cream. When my grandkids sit on Santa's lap in the mall, they have yet to ask Santa how he's doing, if maybe he's getting a little tired of all these kids. They hop on his lap, recite their list of desired gifts, and hop off. We Christians call it prayer.

Petitionary prayers that are offered with no real thought of getting to know God through relational prayer eventually become the rantings of a spoiled brat. Legitimate desires become expectations that slide into the entitlements of perceived necessity. Or, as one friend puts it more simply, dreams become demands.

Our eyes see little more than the sugar cereal that tastes so good. Perhaps we ask for good health or a decent income or powerful ministry, or maybe something illegitimate that we rationalize as good because it promises deep satisfaction—such as a man or woman other than our spouse or the chance to be a hero. The devil stacks the shelves with tasty items, and, in our flesh, we pray, "Give me this. I want that. In Jesus's name and for His glory, amen."

We ask God to heal a sick child, improve our marriage, make us more loving spouses, lift our depression, bring fruit from our ministry, get us a job, make our small group a safe place, make us safe persons in our small group, give us close friends, equip us to be a close friend, lead us to a church where we can belong and serve. So many of our requests are good and legitimate. Some are truly other-centered.

But we're still asking for things without really knowing who it is we're talking to, so we can't really hear His voice. We're aware of our desire for second things—our fulfillment, our satisfaction, our enjoyment of life— and oblivious to God's desire for relationship with us. We hear only ourselves and hope He's listening. Even when He grants a few requests, we feel no deep desire to know Him, no more than a child wants to know Santa Claus. Just stay on good terms with Him (Is this legalism? pressure?) so the goodies keep coming. Let the Giver stop giving, and we throw a tantrum. We think of it as fervent prayer.

THE PURPOSE OF PRAYER IS RELATIONSHIP

So what does all this have to do with getting ready to learn the PAPA prayer? Simply this: we will neither enjoy the PAPA prayer nor flow with its rhythm like a child finally taking off on his two-wheeler until we realize that the chief purpose of prayer is not to get things from God. Neither is it to praise or thank Him from a distance. *The chief purpose of prayer is to get to know God,* to deepen our relationship with Him, to nourish the life of God He's already placed within us, and to do it all to satisfy His desire for relationship with us.

It's not all about us. And it's not only about God. Because of who He is, prayer (and for that matter, the whole Christian life) is all about God and us. It's about our relationship. That's how God wants it. Therefore, it makes sense to say that we must learn to pray relationally, to enjoy a two-way conversation with God where He gets the first and last word, before we ask Him for what we want.

And that's how Jesus taught us to pray. He gave us a model, not merely to repeat but to guide us in our conversations with Papa. We'll look at that model in the next chapter.

chapter seven

This Is No Gimmick—It's a Way to Relate

*W*e're most familiar with the Lord's Prayer in the words of the King James Version:

> Our Father which art in heaven,
> Hallowed be thy name.
> Thy kingdom come.
> Thy will be done in earth, as it is in heaven.
> Give us this day our daily bread,
> And forgive us our debts, as we forgive our debtors.
> And lead us not into temptation, but deliver us from evil:
> For thine is the kingdom, and the power, and the glory, for ever.
> Amen. (Matthew 6:9–13)

There are a few things about that prayer I want you to notice. They're easily overlooked. Start with the very first words: "Our Father." They get us thinking about relationship. "Papa, we're coming to You."

And Jesus wants us to be crystal-clear about who it is we're coming to. Our Papa is the holy God of heaven. If it weren't for Jesus, we'd never even imagine conversing with God and calling Him Papa. Rather, the scene would resemble a courtroom. We'd be standing in the dock trembling before an inflexibly righteous judge, knowing we were about to justly receive the sentence of death.

But Jesus has changed everything. We're now the president's children with free access to the Oval Office, able to climb up in our Papa's lap while He commands armies across the world in the real war against terror.

As we listen from our cozy vantage point, we begin to understand what our heavenly Papa is up to. With relaxed confidence and invincible authority, He is bringing heaven's kingdom to earth. It takes a while, but eventually it dawns on us that He is intent on reproducing in our human relationships the kind of community He has always enjoyed with His Son and Spirit.

We see the glint in His eye, the firm set of His jaw, and we realize He means business. His kingdom will come to earth, and no power can stop it. We're still not sure what it all means, but a fiery excitement rises within us. "Papa, may it happen. May Your kingdom fill the earth."

He looks down at us with the affirming expression of a coach sending his star player onto the field. And we realize we have a part in making it happen. *Me? I have a part? But who am I? What's going on in me? What can I do?*

We cry out, "Give me the bread I need to strengthen me to carry out Your mission." With His bread and His mission on our minds, we realize we really don't need our son to turn his life around or our spouse to love us well. We don't need to fully recover from the recent stroke we suffered. We don't even need a job in order to do our part in showing others the way God relates to people. All we need is bread from heaven, the bread of life. We want those other blessings, but they're all second things. We don't need them to satisfy the deepest desire of God's heart and ours, or to achieve our mission.

All that is true. We don't always think that way, but when we do, we see that second things have become first in our affections. And our prayer life has been all about petitioning God to give us those second things. That realization leads to purging.

We pray, "Papa, I've not valued You as I should. Like the prodigal, I've wanted Your resources at my disposal more than I've wanted You. I'm actually willing to not be with You if it means I could have everything else I want and just feel good. That's awful! Forgive me. I'm not worthy to sit on Your lap.

"And I've been so intent on filling up my emptiness through others that I've been holding grudges against people who haven't come through for me. That's awful too. Papa, forgive me as I now forgive them."

Then, with a clearer focus on who our Papa is and what He's up to, and with a humbling awareness of who we are and what we've been up to, we recognize that a battle is raging in our hearts. But it's a subtle war, a hidden one. It's difficult for us to see where the front lines are and what the fight is all about.

But one thing is clear. We know there is something in us that's attracted to the idea of promoting our kingdom, of doing whatever we can to change our spouse to treat us as we want to be treated, and of protecting ourselves from looking or feeling bad in all our relationships. And yet we say, "Thy will be done, in this relationship, in the middle of this argument." That's what we want to want. But we're not there.

A woman told a friend whose husband hasn't a clue how to connect with her heart that she ought to consider leaving him. "He has no right to treat you that way. Find your own voice. Treat yourself as the woman of dignity that you are. Let him know you won't stand for the shabby way he treats you any longer."

The woman who gave that advice should fall on her knees and pray, "Lead me not into temptation. Deliver me from the evil one." She believed the devil's lie. She was thinking from a lower perspective, a perspective that places her satisfaction and the satisfaction of her friend as the measure of what is right. When she talked with the hurting wife, Christ wasn't pouring out of her life. Wisdom from hell slithered out of her mouth. And it so easily slithers out of mine. We must all pray, "Oh Papa, deliver us from evil."

Now we're praying with the mind of Christ. We're praying the Lord's prayer. We're relating to God, we're drawing close, and now He's drawing close to us. That's what Jesus had in mind when He said, "If anyone loves me [relationship], he will obey my teaching [the fruit of relationship]. My Father will love him [He already does, but He'll make His love felt], and we [both Papa and Jesus by their Spirit] will come to him and make our home with him" (John 14:23).

FOLLOWING JESUS'S EXAMPLE OF PRAYER

The Lord's Prayer shows us how to pray in a way that honors the purpose of prayer. It moves us toward abiding in Christ, toward becoming aware of His life in us, with its heavenly rhythm and purpose. First things and second things begin to sort themselves out, and we pray differently. We want different things. We want what God wants. And we pray in the Spirit, as Christ did.

That makes us a little more like Jesus. We realize that what we want most is a close relationship with our Papa, and we ask for whatever we need to carry out His will.

And Jesus not only taught us how to pray, but He showed us how to pray. Never once did He place priority value on anything that would put distance between Him and His Father. Of course He wanted a good meal after His forty-day fast, but not if it would distance Him one inch from His Father. And if using His resources to protect Himself kept His Father's kingdom from being displayed, He didn't use them. In Gethsemane, He asked to be spared the cross centrally because He knew His Father would turn away from Him as He hung there. That prospect terrified Him far more than the nails.

Even there, in Gethsemane, He trusted His Father with all His troubles. Their relationship, a brutally honest one, was everything to Him. Like any other human being, Jesus didn't relish the prospect of torture. Unlike any other human being, He was prepared to experience the agony of ultimate loneliness because (and I'd never dare say this if it wasn't clearly said in Scripture) it pleased the Father to bruise Him (Isaiah 53:10). Never was the Father pleased to bruise anyone else. No one else's pain could get us into the family where God could reveal Himself as our Papa.

Christ's relationship with His Father was the driving passion behind every request He made. Relationship preceded petition. His life is a profound demonstration of the point I've been making: that getting God is worth infinitely more than getting the things we want from God.

Yet preachers all across America, and especially on television, teach us that Christianity is about gaining God's favor in our lives, that by confident and persistent prayer we can have the blessings we want. They are false prophets.

The PAPA Prayer Is Not a Formula to Manipulate God

One more thing. I suppose it's clear by now that I am offering the PAPA prayer as a way to develop your relationship with God. But I would rather have you burn this book and warn everyone you meet against it than to have you read it and think the PAPA prayer is a slick gimmick or formula for getting close to God. Nothing we do makes Him do anything. We can only present ourselves to God, attend to our experience of Him, purge ourselves by admitting wrong ways of relating we are powerless to change, and then approach God for mercy. But we want more. We want something that works, that puts us in control, that gives us power to make things happen.

As a result, we are committed to "thing-ism." Come up with a good idea, market the dickens out of it, and pray it becomes the latest thing.

Whether it's a new method of prayer or the latest popular author or conference speaker, we love to get on board. Whatever it is, it promises to change our lives. That's the appeal.

Recently I worshiped with some younger evangelicals in Irvine, California, at New Song Church. It was a wonderful experience. I came away deeply grateful for how disillusioned younger people are with the never-ending wave of new things we older evangelicals systematize and shamelessly promote with ridiculous promises that have no biblical warrant whatsoever.

Let me speak clearly: I do not recommend the PAPA prayer as a way to make anyone more spiritual. To do so would deny both the Spirit's free sovereignty and our freedom to flow with or resist His movement when it comes. We can make nothing that deeply matters turn out the way we want. So we must keep doing what we can, what we believe we're directed to do, but not to make anything happen. We are to do what's right with a growing awareness of our poverty and dependence. The rest is up to Papa. That's obedience. That's trust. That's humility.

Praying the PAPA prayer has helped me feel less powerful. I sense deeper brokenness when I realize how strongly I don't want God's kingdom to come if it interferes with the arrival of my kingdom. That becomes clear when I look at the motives that direct how I sometimes relate to people I love. And then I realize that my weakness and brokenness are God's opportunity to release His life more fully through me.

And as that happens, I get to know Him, and myself, a little better. I like that. If you have a way to pray that better gets you in touch with your emptiness and God's sufficiency, follow it. But if your prayer life feels like a child sitting on Santa's lap, making a lot of requests of someone you really don't know, then this book might be God's message for you.

The PAPA prayer is a way to experience what Jesus had in mind when

He said that if we remain in Him and if His word remains in us, then we could ask for whatever we wanted and He would give it to us.

He meant what He said. A few thoughts on those words from John 15:7, and then we'll be ready to learn the PAPA prayer.

chapter eight

Stay at Home with Christ

$\mathcal{A}$ friend just called. Her husband has never known how to deeply connect with her. And he wasn't bothering to learn. It had been a long journey for her through some pretty dark nights, but she had faced the real battle going on in her soul: would she demand he move toward her and then retreat if he didn't, perhaps into divorce? Or would she firmly shove her happiness as a wife into second place and get to know God well enough to bring heaven's kingdom into her marriage by relating to her husband with Christ's energy?

That was her choice: the Spirit or the flesh? The kingdom of light or the kingdom of darkness? Her heavenly Papa or the father of lies? She had come to see that enduring the marriage with no thought of revealing God's character to her husband was no less sinful than ending it. And she realized that praying for her husband to change could no longer be the center of her prayer life.

She was slowly learning to relax in her Papa's arms, to value closeness with Him more than closeness with her husband, and to eat enough daily bread to keep her focused on trickling Christ out of her life toward her husband rather than protecting herself from him.

I heard a fresh excitement in her voice. "Larry, he said he'd talk with you. I felt a softness in him I've never felt before. Could you see him?"

I was both thrilled and alarmed. People who stay close to Christ often see good things happen. Spouses warm up. Obnoxious teenagers get polite. Headaches go away. And celebration is called for. I felt eager to seize the opportunity. If God could use me to help this guy love his wife better, I'd be delighted. When second-thing blessings come, throw a party. Enjoy how good you feel.

But second-thing blessings can feel so good that we start thinking they're the first thing. Listen to God talking to Israel about getting into the Promised Land: "When you have eaten and are satisfied, praise the LORD your God for the good land he has given you." In other words, celebrate your blessings. But "be careful that you do not forget the LORD your God, failing to observe his commands. . . . Otherwise, when you eat and are satisfied [i.e., when your husband starts loving you well] . . . you will forget the LORD your God, who brought you out . . . of slavery" (Deuteronomy 8:10–14).

In this life, the feeling of satisfaction that comes when a marriage improves or a child turns back to God or an inheritance solves our financial problems or a ministry takes off often feels stronger and brings more pleasure than our experience of God. We are foolish to dampen that pleasure, but we are in danger of living for it, of thinking that blessings from God satisfy our souls more deeply than God Himself.

The problem, of course, is that our relationship with God is so shallow that the pleasure it brings really is less than the pleasure we feel when life goes well. That was one reason for my alarm.

There was a second. The difficult truth is that relationship with God, this side of heaven, does not always feel good. Living for God, sincerely and sacrificially, does not always generate the pleasurable experience of meaning and joy. God lets us experience seasons of emptiness and futility that simply cannot be endured if our real aim is satisfaction in this life.

Jesus's greatest moment of surrender came when He faced His most terrifying prospect of aloneness. And that surrender released His deepest resolve. The tortures of Gethsemane prepared Him for the unspeakable horrors of Calvary. Without wrestling in the Garden, would He have found the strength to remain on the cross?

I don't know. But I do know that when the terror of abandonment that He faced in Gethsemane became a reality on Calvary, He cried out in pain never before experienced and then, with His last breath, gave Himself in total trust to His Father.

Remaining faithful in relationship to God sometimes produces agony in our souls that only compromise can relieve. It was these thoughts that made me concerned for my friend. Would she be deceived into valuing the prospect of her husband's satisfying movement toward her more than her unfelt relationship with Papa? Would she turn from worship to idolatry and not even realize it was happening? Would her prayers of petition yield to prayers of thanksgiving that might nudge aside prayers of relationship with God from their central place?

What Does It Mean to "Pray in the Spirit"?

Jesus addressed this concern. He told us to remain in Him, to stay at home with God and not settle down in the comfortable world of blessings. And He added, "If you remain in me, then I'll give you whatever you ask." The power of petitionary prayer, He seems to be saying, depends on the priority of relational prayer.

Let's look at this passage and explore it a bit. Here's how Eugene Peterson renders it in *The Message*: "I am the Vine, you are the branches. When you're joined with me and I with you, the relation intimate and organic, the harvest is sure to be abundant. Separated, you can't produce a thing. Anyone who separates from me is deadwood [remember, He's talking to believers] gathered up and thrown on the bonfire [of no use to kingdom purposes]. But if you make yourselves at home with me and my words are at home in you, you can be sure that whatever you ask will be listened to and acted upon" (John 15:5–7).

In this short passage, Jesus is introducing an entirely different approach to prayer than the one we naturally follow. What do the prayers look like of people who remain in Christ, who make themselves at home with Jesus, and who feel at home with everything He says? What does it mean to "pray in the Spirit"?

Jude uses that phrase in verse 20 of his one-chapter book. And he follows it by saying, "Keep yourselves in God's love" (v. 21). Is Jude implying that God could stop loving us if we don't behave in certain ways? Of course not. We're loved; we couldn't be loved more, and we'll never be loved less.

But we can choose to leave love's party because it doesn't always feel like a party. Like a cool '50s teenager, we can sneak away from the dance and smoke a cigarette with a couple of buddies out back. It is possible, and epidemically common, to move away from the reality of God's love and to remain in ourselves, self-obsessed and concerned with nothing more than our experience of fullness and satisfaction.

We do it every time we live for second things. We do it every time we pray harder for our marriage to feel better than we pray to more closely relate with God. We do it every time we pray more for personal blessings to make our lives happier than to bear fruit for the sake of God's kingdom.

And when we remain in self and lose awareness of Papa's love, we can't pray in the Spirit. The only prayer God hears from one of His kids who is living in rebellion, who constantly values second things above God, is one version of the PAPA prayer: "God, here I am. I know You love me. I've been more concerned with feeling better about myself and wanting life to go better than being with You. I'm coming home. Will You have me?" That prayer returns our hearts to Christ and then allows us to remain in Him.

If we remain in self, if we're not drawing on God's love as the most treasured reality in our lives, we'll treasure something else—and we'll pray for it. It may never cross our minds that we're praying for a second thing, that we're using God, even trying to control Him, more than worshiping Him. The danger is especially great when the thing we're praying for is a promised perk of the spiritual life.

Listen to this warning from Oswald Chambers: "We utilize God for the sake of getting peace and joy, that is, we do not realize Jesus Christ, but only our enjoyment of Him. This is the first step in a wrong direction."[1]

Do we see the danger Chambers's finger is on? It's very subtle. Jesus Christ does satisfy our souls, but not always right away. Sometimes we have to trust that one day, not now, we'll know beyond doubt that God's requirement to remain in Him perfectly aligns with the deepest desire of our hearts. In the moment, however, giving priority to our relationship with God may not produce the maximum satisfaction in our souls that we legitimately desire.[2]

If we value our satisfaction in Christ more than Christ Himself, we remain committed to ourselves and not Christ. We may think we're committed to Him, and in a sense we are—but only as a means to an end. The end is not Christ's glory; the end is our satisfaction.

We may think we're worshiping God and praying in the Spirit when all we're doing is using Him, as a woman who wants a baby might use a man to gain what she believes is her greatest good. The fruit of the relationship is more treasured than the relationship itself. When the provider fails to provide, when the woman doesn't get pregnant, or when the joy isn't felt, the temptation to look elsewhere to gain what we want becomes irresistible. Or we pray harder to win the provision from the provider. And relational prayer means nothing.

FOCUS ON THE PROVIDER, NOT THE PROVISION

Jesus warns us against this danger. If we focus on what we need (provision) more than the One we come to with our needs (the provider), we'll "keep on babbling like pagans" (Matthew 6:7). We'll endlessly petition God for things He already knows we need, and, worse, we'll try to come up with a way to pray that we hope will persuade or even obligate God to come through for us.

Jesus had a better idea: "Here's what I want you to do: Find a quiet, secluded place so you won't be tempted to role-play before God. Just be there as simply and honestly as you can manage. The focus will shift from you to God, and you will begin to sense his grace. The world is full of so-called prayer warriors who are prayer-ignorant. They're full of formulas and programs and advice, peddling techniques for getting what you want from God. Don't fall for that nonsense. This is your Father you are dealing with, and he knows better than you what you need. With a God like this loving you, you can pray very simply" (Matthew 6:6–9 MSG).

Then He gave us the Lord's Prayer, which I discussed in the preceding chapter. What I hear Him saying is, stop babbling all your requests as if God needs persuading to be generous. As Archbishop Trench once said, "We must not conceive of prayer as an overcoming of God's reluctance, but a laying hold of His highest willingness."[3] Get to know your heavenly Papa. Realize He's unapproachably holy and lives far away in heaven, but He is closer to you right now than you are to yourself.

Focus on what's going on in heaven, where three divine Persons are having a great time together. Realize how much they want you to join the fun and share it with others, even with cold, distant husbands. Think about what your Papa's love would look like coming out of you in your marriage, with your kids, in your small group.

Then ask for something. Ask God for the power to pull it off, to bring heaven's kingdom to earth in your relationships, not to change people you're relating with so that your needs are better met. As you realize how poorly you're doing that, ask again, this time for forgiveness. You're looking for soul satisfaction, which is only available in God, through others. That's both foolish and wrong. When you realize how foolish and wrong you are, you'll value Jesus and the cross more than ever. The passion of Christ will become more than a great movie. It will take its rightful place at the center of your life.

And you'll discover a new power to forgive others (cold husbands, rejecting wives, pain-in-the-neck teenagers, insensitive friends), but you'll feel the struggle. So you'll add one more request. You'll ask to be delivered from the one person in all the world who most wants you to hold on to your grudge and live like a citizen of self's kingdom, where your interests come first.

That's praying in the Spirit. That's remaining in Christ. As I write these words, I have to contain my excitement. I want to shout, "Do it! It's unbelievable!" Do it enough, and you'll start experiencing the power to resist your favorite private sin. Do it enough, and you'll still hurt when you're treated poorly, but you'll count it a privilege to suffer with Christ and, like Him, to cling to your Papa. You'll know His power to bring the way He lives (His kingdom) into your relationships.

The truth is that I've had moments of praying in the Spirit. I've known what it means to be so aware of God's love, so amazed, that when Papa walks up the stairs and sees me, He starts singing with delight. And some of His life and love have actually trickled out of me into others. Amazing!

The acid test, by the way, of whether it's really Papa's life trickling out of you or a counterfeit is whether it trickles most toward the people closest to you, those who can be the most difficult to love. It's much easier for me to pour patient kindness into a client I see occasionally than into my family. I demand more from my family than I do from clients.

The trickle of God's life (perhaps someday it will turn into a river) comes out of me only when I relate to God before I request from God. When I do, I know what it means to pray in the Spirit. I pray for first things with confidence and for second things with relaxed hope.

But I have a dickens of a time keeping myself in God's love. How can I do that?

REMAIN IN CHRIST

Our Lord invited us to make ourselves "at home" with Him, to remain in Him (John 15:7 MSG). The closest picture I can form of that is sitting with my wife on the back deck on a warm, summer evening or in two comfortable chairs in front of our fireplace on a snowy, January night. The thought of asking her for something is not on my mind. Enjoying her is. The point is being together.

When I feel "at home" with my wife, whatever desires do come to my mind never violate our togetherness. Being with her means more to me than what I might get from her. In that moment, nothing I might want would occur to me that would not be what she would want as well.

And that's a picture for me of what John wrote: "This is the confidence we have in approaching God: that if we ask anything according to his will, he hears us. And if we know that he hears us—whatever we ask—we know that we have what we asked of him" (1 John 5:14–15).

As I sit with my wife, I sense what she wants the most. And that's what I ask for. She gives it every time. It's the same with God.

Relational prayer is the condition for power in petitionary prayer. Why? Relational prayer changes what we most fervently ask for, and it dissolves our spirit of entitlement when we request anything. James said that when we ask with wrong motives, even for good things, we will not get them. I think he is warning us to check out whether the ultimate object of our petitionary prayer is our satisfaction. If it is, then we're not at home with Christ.

Remaining in Christ requires us to focus on three things: (1) the value of what Christ has done for us that we could never do for ourselves—namely, getting us adopted into Papa's family; (2) our radical helplessness to arrange for our satisfaction or to do something of real significance without daily bread from Him; (3) our need to spend time being with God in silence and solitude. That may include a weekend away at a retreat center, but it need not. Our inner world can become a monastery where we sit with God in the middle of a busy life.

But don't let that thought justify your driven busyness. If I wave a warm good-bye to my wife as I run to catch my next plane, yet I never take the time to sit and talk with her, I will not be remaining with her.

So, to sum up, remaining in Christ means that we consciously, every day, value Him as our source of life and stop demanding anyone else fill us up. It means that we depend on Him for everything good coming out of us and that we want His goodness coming out of us into others more than we want His goodness coming out of others into us. And it means that we pay whatever price is required and sacrifice whatever ambition we must in order to draw close to Him, to experience a level of union that arouses our awareness of His life within us.

That's relational prayer.

chapter nine

&

How I'm Learning to Pray

I earlier described what each letter in PAPA stands for:

Present yourself to God.
Attend to how you are thinking of God.
Purge yourself of anything that blocks your relationship with God.
Approach God as the "first thing" in your life.

In part 2, I'll develop each part thoroughly and practically, so you will know how to pray the PAPA prayer, but let me briefly tell you how I do it. I offer the next few paragraphs less as instruction and more as illustration. Only the Lord's Prayer has biblical warrant to serve as a model for prayer. And the recorded prayers of Paul, especially in Ephesians, are far better illustrations than what I can give. The PAPA prayer is simply my way of trying to follow the model of Jesus and the example of Paul. And the way I do it is the wobbly way a child rides his first two-wheeler.

PRESENT YOURSELF TO GOD

First, I *present myself to God.* That's the first *P* in PAPA. I begin as Jesus taught us to begin, with the realization I'm talking to the holy God who invites me to call Him Father. So I often say, "Father, if it weren't for grace, You couldn't stand the sight of me. But Jesus died, so here I come. I'm believing that You're sitting on the floor wanting me to be with You."

Before I make any requests, I reflect on what's going on in me at that moment. That doesn't come naturally.

I met Mary for lunch today. I know she's hurting. On the way to the restaurant, I began praying for her. "God, bless our time together. May Mary come to know You better."

I caught myself asking for something in religious language, and I stopped. I was asking before relating. And it felt more appropriate than real. I wasn't coming as I was to be with God. So I began noticing what was happening in me as I was on my way to meet Mary. I appreciate her. She never makes me feel like I owe her time. I see a deep spirit of humility in her. I feel privileged to be meeting with her and long to walk with her into her heart, where the speaking Spirit lives.

So I told God that. He didn't learn anything He didn't already know, but somehow I felt closer to Him. We were relating as friends, and I think it helped me be more present to Mary.

Presenting myself to God is that simple. I tell Him who I am in the moment, as much as I can see without obsessing about myself or probing the depths of my unconscious. I figure the Spirit will eventually bring to mind what He wants me to see that's hidden if I make a habit of presenting myself to Him.

ATTEND TO HOW YOU ARE THINKING OF GOD

Then, I *attend* (the first *A* in PAPA) *to whatever I am experiencing that I think might be God.* Am I aware of His presence? When was I most recently aware that He was present to me? What about Him seems real and alive right now? Anything? Sometimes nothing seems real.

Do I see Him as my sovereign Lord before whom I have no rights, only mercy-granted privileges? Or do I regard God as a cosmic vending machine with buttons I can press to get whatever I want?

My one rule is never to pretend, never to convince myself that I'm aware of something supernatural when I'm not or that I'm petitioning the Almighty God when I'm really snapping my fingers for the butler to bring me coffee. And I do my best not to use religious language, to stay away from those flowery phrases Christians sometimes use to stir up counterfeit emotions that are not the fruit of experiencing God Himself.

For example, I don't say, "O Wonderful God, my lover and my friend, the awesome triune God, I gratefully embrace Your presence with me." Some people might be able to speak like that with authenticity. I can't. It feels contrived. And that creates distance between God and me.

I'm more apt to say something like, "You seemed really real yesterday, when I was reading Jeremiah 32. And I can sense a quiet thrill that right now You're eager to do me good. You're different than anyone I know. You amaze me"; or, "Right now, You seem indifferent, kind of impatient with how slowly I'm growing."

PURGE YOURSELF OF ANYTHING THAT BLOCKS YOUR RELATIONSHIP WITH GOD

Third, I *purge myself of anything that blocks my relationship with God.* That's the second *P* in PAPA. When I think about God, I can't help thinking about myself. And that's good; it's relational. But when I'm thinking about God, I tend not to think of myself in flattering terms. As John Piper has said, "No man stands on the edge of the Grand Canyon and says, 'Aren't I something!'"

I feel small but real when I stand before God. I'm there, I exist, but I'm humbled. When people met God in the Scripture, they often fell flat on their faces. That's real. It's what happens when you face the way things really are. Because I understand sin to be valuing something more than God and because I'm still sinful, I typically become aware of what I want right then more than I want God. There's always something. I can't get through a minute without thinking life is more about me and my satisfaction than about God and His glory.

One of my besetting sins is my demand that someone be more interested in hearing me than in me hearing them. I'm good at asking questions. And while I'm drawing people out, I secretly feel superior and angry because I'm being curious about them, but they're not curious about me. They can tell me their problems, but I'm allowed to share mine only if it helps them. That's one of my favorite gripes: "I wish someone would let me talk about my life the way I'm going to let Mary talk about hers today."

So I tell God, rarely without a fight, that I can see my griping as self-centered, self-protective sin. It certainly isn't the kind of sacrificial love Jesus modeled. His disciples fell asleep while He was crying, and He instructed them in godly living and then died for them so they could follow His instructions, for their well-being and His Father's pleasure.

Purging, as I see it, means more than just telling God what I see is going on in me that might be dulling my experience of Him. But it means less than getting rid of it. I can't do that.

However, I can recognize that saying yes to immediate satisfaction is often a way of saying no to trusting God with the hope that deeper satisfaction is available in Him. I'm filling up my empty stomach with junk food, so I have no appetite when the chef brings out the steak. That's foolishness. Worse, it's idolatry. I want someone to listen to me! Does anyone give a rip how my life is going? Do I matter to anyone?

And when I see it for what it is, when I see my cry for satisfaction as unholy desire, as self-obsession, I bow before God in brokenness—which is the proper position for listening.

Approach God As the "First Thing" in Your Life

Then I'm ready to *approach God* (the last letter in PAPA, the second *A*) by acknowledging that He is my greatest good, my *summum bonum*. The first three parts of the prayer (presenting, attending, and purging) free me to tell God I really do want Him to be first in my life—the first thing in my thinking, the first thing in my affections, the first thing in my purposes, and the first thing in my choices. I want to trust Him with my satisfaction by devoting my life to His pleasure.

It then becomes clear that everything else is a second thing. Whether my spouse makes me feel important, whether my lunch mate asks me more than one question, whether my cancer comes back, whether I feel alive and vital and full of excitement—everything I want besides God is a second thing, legitimate in its place but an idol if it climbs into a higher place than God and His glory.

As I drove to meet Mary, I prayed, "God, I long to be free from the need to help her. The first thing is to rest in You, to trust You, to please You, and to reflect to her who You are and what You're like. I want Mary to be helped, and I'd love to be helpful, but those are second things. I can sense my desire for You to be first in my life, to hear Your voice telling me that I'm Yours, that You're mine, and that I can pour Your life into Mary as we talk today."

That's a quick illustration, one simple story of how I pray the PAPA prayer. I think that's the first time I've ever publicly made known how I pray. In an earlier chapter, I shared one reason that I've so rarely talked about prayer: I don't want to give the impression that I think my first-grade discussion of prayer should be heard as a graduate course taught by a learned professor.

There's another reason. None of us really knows how to pray. Paul said as much in Romans 8:26: "We do not know what we ought to pray for, but the Spirit himself intercedes for us with groans that words cannot express."

After we've studied our hardest and thought our best, prayer—especially petitionary prayer—will remain a mystery. But if we learn to present ourselves, attend to who we think we're talking to, purge ourselves of whatever is blocking us from enjoying the privilege of keeping company with God, and approach God as our most wonderful treasure, then prayer—though still a mystery—will become a delight. We'll be relating to the One who knows us best and loves us most.

chapter ten

&

A New Paradigm for Prayer

*W*e've now completed our preparations and are ready to learn the PAPA prayer. The preparation was long because the shift from our usual way of praying will be radical. The shift is finding a way to put relational prayer in the exact center of our prayer life.

If we don't pray relationally (to know God, to move toward union with God so that we increasingly experience His life in us and pour His life out of us into others) before we start asking for things, we'll become narcissists disguised as Jesus followers, and we won't realize what we've become. Prayer will be the weakest part of our spiritual journey.

TWO PARADIGMS OF PRAYER

As I look at how people pray, including myself, I see two basic paradigms. A paradigm is a way of viewing things; it is a general understanding of a subject that shapes how we think about that subject and how we deal with it in our daily lives.

The paradigm that is far more commonly accepted among Christians today is what I call the "Get Things from God" paradigm. What's the point of prayer? Well, to get something from God He might be willing to give. And that something usually is a blessing that, if given, will make our lives more comfortable. A better job, more money, a loving spouse, expanded ministry—the list is long. So we pray much. We babble on.

There is another way. The second paradigm for prayer, anticipated by the prophets (see especially Habakkuk), taught by Jesus, and practiced by Paul, sees prayer as a unique opportunity to get to know God better, to surrender gladly to His will and to depend on the Spirit to advance His will through our way of relating to others. We might call it the "Get to Know God Better" paradigm for prayer.

In this view, prayer is centered in relational prayer. All other varieties flow out of prayer that deepens our relationship with God, and they are in perfect rhythm with that relationship.

For subscribers to this second paradigm, worship and praise not only continue during hard times, but they deepen. It becomes clear that worship is the passion to sacrifice every second thing for the first thing of knowing God. Praise is directed first toward God's name and then toward His benefits. The psalmist sang, "Praise the LORD, O my soul; all my inmost being, praise his holy name." Then he added, "And forget not all his benefits" (Psalm 103:1–2).

Praise fastens on hope. Everything will be all right—later, not now. But Papa is here now. Nothing can go wrong that will not one day be straightened—not Parkinson's, not rape, not bankruptcy, not even moral failure. So we praise in hope more passionately than we beg for change.

From relational prayer flows true petitionary prayer. Out of both come worship and praise, and confession and lament. As we own our faults and struggle with pain, we open the door, not to fewer temptations and more pleasant circumstances but to knowing God better, to receiving His tender mercies and limitless compassion. We get to know Him better.

This paradigm does exactly what it says; it provides an understanding of prayer that lets us know God better. And we discover we want nothing more. It takes time, but it happens for everyone who learns to relationally pray: we know God better, and we rest, not in fullness but in hope of fullness.

SHIFTING OUR PARADIGM OF PRAYER

This book is a call to shift our paradigm of prayer. After buying into the wrong one for so long and living in a Christian culture that promotes and assumes it in a thousand ways, the shift may be difficult. For many of us, it's a new paradigm. It may be a brand-new thought—and a radical one— that prayer is getting more of God rather than getting more from God.

The first step in shifting our paradigm of prayer from a familiar to an unfamiliar one is to clearly see the difference in the two and to be convinced that one is wrong and one is right. Let me conclude part 1 by lining up the eight assumptions of the "Get to Know God Better" paradigm next to the eight assumptions people make when they pray according to the "Get Things from God" paradigm.

I urge you to think carefully about these two sets of assumptions. When you see the radical difference between the two paradigms and realize how self-focused the "getting things" paradigm is, you'll be ready to learn the PAPA prayer.

The "Get to Know God Better" Paradigm	The "Get Things from God" Paradigm
Assumption #1 Prayer is more about us hearing God than about Him hearing us. We're the audience.	**Assumption #1** Prayer is an opportunity to get God to hear our requests. He's our audience.

The "Get to Know God Better" Paradigm (cont'd)	The "Get Things from God" Paradigm (cont'd)
Assumption #2 Real prayer is never dull. We aren't praying unless prayer is the most vital thing we do, whether we receive what we ask for or not.	**Assumption #2** Excitement in prayer depends on receiving what we ask for, or at least on the hope that we will.
Assumption #3 Prayer is the God-appointed means for us to come to know Him as Papa.	**Assumption #3** Prayer is the God-appointed means for us to receive what we need in order to feel satisfaction and fulfillment.
Assumption #4 Prayer can become the conversation you longed to have with your earthly father. As that happens, your "father wounds" are healed.	**Assumption #4** Prayer consists of asking things from God in a way that releases Him to treat us like children who are entitled to their inheritance.
Assumption #5 Power in petitionary prayer depends on intimacy in relational prayer. Know God a little, and experience little power in petition. Know God a lot and experience great power in petition.	**Assumption #5** Power in petitionary prayer depends on visible passion, declared faith, length of prayer, number of prayers, and perhaps posture.

The "Get to Know God Better" Paradigm (cont'd)	The "Get Things from God" Paradigm (cont'd)
Assumption #6 Petitioning God without first relating to Him transforms legitimate desire into entitled demands.	**Assumption #6** Prayer is our way of holding God to His promises. We have a right to approach God, knowing we are entitled to what He has promised.
Assumption #7 Prayer is not a technique for persuading a reluctant God to give us what we want. It is our primary opportunity to get acquainted with God in this life before we see Him in the next.	**Assumption #7** Prayer is a method for securing blessings now that we will receive in full measure later.
Assumption #8 Knowing God changes what we most want in this life, and that changes what we most fervently request.	**Assumption #8** God grants the desires of our hearts. Therefore, we should discern what we believe would bring us the most satisfaction, and ask for that.

Present yourself to God.

"God, I'm feeling excited about the possibility of knowing You better."

Attend to how you are thinking of God.

"I see You as more eager to be close to me than I am to be close to You. I love that."

Purge yourself of anything that blocks your relationship with God.

"But the desire to change some things in my life is really strong. I know that's OK. But I think it's stronger right now than my desire to know You better. And that's not OK. I don't know how to change that."

Approach God as the "first thing" in your life.

"So I come to You just as I am. I don't know what else to do. But I believe You'll do the work and You'll show me my part. I want to know You more than I want anything else."

You've just prayed the PAPA prayer. Now let's think more carefully about how you can pray that prayer for the rest of your life.

part two

Learning to Pray
THE PAPA PRAYER

chapter eleven

∝

It's Time to Learn the PAPA Prayer

$\mathcal{W}$e can move God, but only if we know Him. The better we know Him (and I mean know Him, not just know about Him), the more we'll be excited about what He's up to, what He wants to do in us and in others. As that excitement guides our prayers, we'll see more of our prayers answered. So the key is to know God. Knowing God is the key to everything.

All that you've just read in part 1 has a twofold purpose:

First, I introduced a simple but revolutionary idea that could radically alter the way we pray. It could make prayer the most vital and meaningful part of our spiritual lives. The idea is this: *prayer is our opportunity to build a passionate relationship with God, to know Him well.* True prayer has the power to connect what is deepest in our hearts with what is deepest in His and to release His life into us.

Second, I suggested that relating to God is the point of prayer, and petitioning God is one privilege of prayer.

The order matters. Relational prayer must precede petitionary prayer, or we'll be asking God for things in the same way we might write to the president of the United States and ask a personal favor. If we knew him, or better still, if he were our father, our request would have more effect.

First Relate to God, Then Ask for What You Need

We ask well of God only if we first relate well with God. We do not relate well with God when we begin our prayers by tuning in to what we want, to what we believe will fulfill our lives and make us happy, and then going to God to ask for it.

We do relate well with God when we do the four things that build any relationship: get real about who we are with someone we trust, show genuine interest in who that person is, own up to whatever we do that damages the relationship, and honor our relationship with the person as our unrivaled priority.

Translate those same four elements into our relationship with God, and it looks like this:

Present yourself to God authentically; be real with Him as you are with no one else.

Attend to how you are thinking of God, how you picture Him as you're talking to Him, and then modify your perception to fit who He tells you He is.

Purge yourself of your relational faults by taking an inventory of how you put your interests ahead of His and getting rid of anything that blocks intimacy with Him.

Approach God just as you are, tuning in to your passion to know Him and to honor Him above all others.

That's the PAPA prayer. But how do we do it? What does it look like to present, attend, purge, and approach in our conversation with God? That's the question I want to answer in part 2.

Revisiting the Questions

One more thing before we start. When I invited you early in this book to learn the PAPA prayer, I asked you nine questions to pique your interest—nine questions intended to surface whatever frustration you might be experiencing in your prayer life and to whet your appetite for what a new way to pray could do for your relationship with God.

Let me restate those questions here, rephrasing them a bit:

1. Ever pray for something you didn't receive? Has that become a pattern?
2. Ever seek guidance from the Lord that never came? Does God really guide your decisions?
3. Ever try to convince yourself that you heard from God when you really weren't sure you had?
4. Ever wonder if God even knows what you're going through, let alone cares?
5. Ever feel empty and alone, and then felt more empty and alone after you prayed for comfort?
6. Ever ask for strength to resist temptation and feel the temptation get stronger?
7. Do you enjoy God's company? Do you like to pray just to be with God?
8. Do you think it's possible to enjoy His company more than you enjoy anyone else's, and do you want to?
9. Do you connect with God in such a way that you hear His voice and know He's with you, no matter what is happening in your life?

I don't want to promise too much. I don't want to stir up hope that will never be realized, but I do want to say this: if you learn the PAPA prayer, if you enter into this opportunity to know God and stick with it, then I believe that what is happening in my life will happen in yours. You will . . .

- experience new power in petitionary prayer;
- receive unmistakable guidance from God;
- discover that your soul has "ears" that can hear the voice of God;

- enjoy renewed confidence that God is listening to you pray;
- know His presence is real;
- deepen your appetite for God until you want Him more than any other pleasure;
- actually enjoy His company and know He enjoys yours;
- yearn to know Him better until knowing Him will become the point of your life;
- develop confidence that every empty space in your soul will be filled;
- depend on that confidence as your sustaining hope through every trial until you get home.

Well, preparation time is over. Are you ready? Let's learn the PAPA prayer!

PRESENT YOURSELF TO GOD

chapter twelve

C&

Stop Trying to Be Who You Think You Should Be

*E*d and Melanie are friends of mine. Melanie despises Ed.[1]

She recently asked me, "How am I supposed to love him? He thinks only of himself. He'll help with the kids if I ask him a hundred times. I cut the grass and empty the trash. I can't even stand to let him kiss me anymore. I service him sexually every couple of months when I feel guilty over how long it's been, which he, of course, lets me know.

"I know something's terribly wrong with my attitude. I know I'm bitter, but I really don't know what to do. Sometimes after a good sermon or a meaningful time in the Bible, I try to be nicer to him—you know, be warmer, make him a dinner I know he likes. But it never lasts. When I'm nicer, he takes me more for granted. I'm really getting depressed. Any thoughts?"

I replied, "Stop trying so hard to behave the way you think you should."

"Just go ahead and tell him how I really feel? I've tried that too. It makes things worse."

"Pray."

"You think I haven't? Let me tell you, I've prayed. I've been on the floor in tears praying about this. I know I should pray for God to change me, not just him, and I do. But nothing's happening."

"So you're asking God to do something?"

"Yes! To change me. To make me a better wife. I'm so mad, and I know I'm critical. But I can't do whatever it is I'm supposed to do."

"What would it be like for you to relate to God before you ask Him to change you?"

Pause.

"I have no idea what you're talking about."

❖ ❖ ❖

My friend Stan has a terrible relationship with his father. Stan's dad has been a functioning alcoholic since before Stan was born—he kept a steady job, made good money, and was a nice enough guy, only occasionally mean. But his kids never felt like he was there. He was a friendly, drunk ghost.

Stan's mother divorced him when Stan (the youngest of three) went away to college. That was twenty years ago. Stan is now thirty-eight.

His dad is now on his third marriage. Three months ago, he was diagnosed with advanced prostate cancer. Stan learned about it in an e-mail from his dad's current wife. A short e-mail. Stan's older siblings, a brother who's divorced and drinks too much and a single sister whom Stan thinks is a lesbian, won't have anything to do with their father. Neither is a Christian.

"So what do I do? I didn't feel much when I heard Dad had cancer, but the idea he'd go to hell got to me a little. I've prayed about it, and I have felt some nudge to go visit him. Haven't seen him in four years. We talk a few minutes on the phone maybe two, three times a year. He asks about my kids and sends them a Christmas gift every year, so I guess that's something. Maybe the Spirit is leading me to go down there and just love him. I'm not sure. What do you think?"

"Two things occur to me. First, stop trying so hard to be who you think you should be. Sounds like you think Christianity is more about doing the right thing than knowing the right person. Second, as long as you're thinking more about what you should do than about what's going on inside you, I doubt you'll ever clearly hear God's voice leading you. You'll feel some guilt over not seeing your dad now that he's sick, and you'll wonder if it's the Spirit telling you to go. Or you'll mistake your anger toward your dad as the Spirit's leading you to maybe confront him as a way to open him to Christ."

"OK, I can see that, I think. So what should I do? I don't understand what you mean about seeing what's going on in me."

"Pray."

"I have. A lot. Ever since I got that e-mail about Dad's cancer. I've prayed every day, asking to know what God wants me to do. I've even prayed for Dad's salvation. I thought I was getting some direction. Now I'm not so sure."

"That's how you were praying? Asking God for directions?"

"Sure. Something wrong with that?"

"You've got the cart before the horse. Before you ask God for what you want, it's important to relate to Him."

Pause.

"I don't know what you mean."

START BY PRESENTING YOURSELF TO GOD

If you want to learn the PAPA prayer, if you want to relate to God before you ask Him for anything, start by presenting yourself to God.

How do you do that? As you get ready to talk with God, tune in to whatever is going on in you—what you're feeling right now, what thoughts are floating through your mind. Tune in to whatever you can identify, and tell God about it. Tell Him exactly who you are in the moment. Be real with Him. Hold nothing back. Put into words whatever you know is happening in you.

I've presented myself to God by saying, "You seem a million miles away from me. If I had to decide whether You even exist, let alone care, on the basis of what I feel right now, I'd be an atheist." At other times I've said, "I'm so confused right now. I don't have a clue how to lead our small group tonight. I think I'm afraid that I won't be able to move our group toward a really meaningful time." I've also said, "I feel really good right now. Hopeful. Optimistic. Glad to be alive."

That's presenting yourself to God, talking to Him without pretense, being real, telling Him whatever is going on inside you that you can identify when you pause long enough to notice what is going on.

What would it mean for Stan to present himself to God as the first step in relating to Him before He asks God for guidance? What would it mean for Melanie to come to God by presenting herself as she is to Him in the middle of her marital mess? What would it mean for you to present yourself before God as you continue to live your life with its mixed assortment of blessings and problems?

Find Your "Red Dot"

Let me introduce a simple idea that will help answer those questions. I call it the "red dot."

Picture yourself walking into a large shopping mall that you've never been in before. What's the first thing you look for? The directory. And when you find it, your eyes scan across all the rectangles and numbers until you find, what? The red dot that says You Are Here.

You want to know where you are before you enter the maze of directional signs and storefront displays and countless corridors and milling crowds. Something in you knows that it's better to fix your location, to get your bearings, before you start looking for where you want to go.

It's the same on the spiritual journey. We need to know where we are before we try to get where we should be.

"That's not helpful," Melanie might say. "I already know where I am, and I know who I am. I don't need to think any more about it. I'm married to Ed. I have four kids. I want to just run away from all of them. Yes, I'm mad and I'm frustrated. And I'm really discouraged. There, that's where I am. That's my 'red dot.' Now how do I get to this abundant life Jesus promised? That's the question I want answered."

A long time ago, Socrates said the unexamined life was not worth living. I may be wrong, but I don't think he was telling us to analyze and understand all that we feel and all that's happening to us and in us. That's the mistake that therapy sometimes makes.

What the Bible (a higher authority than Socrates) says, and what I think Socrates meant, is that the *unobserved* life is not worth living (see Proverbs 20:5; Hebrews 4:12). Jesus was really ticked off at the Pharisees for looking at only the outside of their lives, seeing nothing there that particularly concerned them, and then moving on with their religion. "The inside of your life is a dirty mess. Observe that, and then you'll realize that your religion is worthless. It has no power to change you; it only covers up what's wrong." (His actual words are recorded in Matthew 23:25–26, but these are pretty close.)

I hear Jesus telling us to take an inside look. See yourself as you really are. Don't take a quick look and then try to change. Reflect on where you are. Talk it over with God. It'll be uncomfortable. It won't make you feel good. But it will make you think more about God.

You'll realize that you need to think about and experience your relationship with God before you worry about anything else, and that the relationship has some real problems. You'll also begin to see how helpless you are. God sees everything. You can change nothing. What will He do? Your focus will shift from yourself to God.

That's what happened in Eden. Adam got himself in deep trouble. His "red dot" was guilt and terror. He had committed a capital offense against God. So he hid behind a tree. He didn't want to stand in his red dot and face God.

Then God showed up for His customary evening stroll through the garden with His friends. Adam had found the tree with the thickest trunk and was trembling behind it. God called out, "Adam, where are you?"

Didn't He know? Couldn't He see Adam quivering behind the tree? I think God was saying something like this: "Adam, I know where you are. I'm aware of your 'red dot.' But until you come out from hiding, we can't have the relationship we both want. I know you're scared. You think that if you observe your situation, if you face the awfulness of what you've done and who you've become, you'll realize I hate you.

"But I don't. I love you. Stop running away from Me. Stand before Me exactly as you are, with neither defenses nor excuses, and then you'll make the unbelievable discovery that I've come up with a way to welcome you back into a better relationship with Me than you've experienced before or even dreamed possible. To enjoy this relationship I offer, you'll need to look deep inside and see what's really going on in you, what you've become, and what terrifies you so much. Then come tell Me about it. I'll take it from there."

The same God who invited Adam to take an inside look and present what he saw to God did the same thing with a crowd of people on a Galilean hillside thousands of years later. Matthew tells us about it in chapter 11 of his Gospel, in verses 28–30.

Jesus was moved by the sight of helpless people hemmed in by problems they couldn't handle and pressured by religious leaders who told them what they should be doing. "Are any of you ready to admit how tired you are? I know you're worn out by trying to live right with a husband who hardly ever make you feel special. You know you aren't doing a very good job of it. And how about all those decisions you face that confuse you? Like whether to visit a sick dad who has failed you miserably. Have you realized yet how worthless your religion is? Are you burned out on all those principles you're supposed to follow, all those recovery techniques that are supposed to make you feel good about yourself and live more happily?

"What's your red dot? Where are you? Come to Me exactly as you are. Stop trying so hard to be good. Admit you're not so good. Admit how disappointed you are in what you've so far experienced of Me. I know you wonder if I even care. Sometimes you've hated Me. Be who you are in My presence. No, it's not a pretty sight. But I've found a way for Me to look at you with excitement. And My Father is singing over you. You won't hear the music till you come out from hiding. Come. Present yourself to Me. I'll walk with you as you present yourself to My Father. It'll be all right. Trust Me."

The first step in learning the PAPA prayer is to stop trying to get where we want to go and to be still long enough to see where we are. But how do we do it? And what can we expect to find when we look inside?

I'll take up those two questions in the next chapter.

chapter thirteen

CR

Enter Your Red Dot—Don't Just Describe It

*M*ost of us are afraid to release authentic passion from our hearts, to put into words what is deepest within us.

My father was an emotionally alive but suppressed man. We loved each other, but we shared very few moments of real encounter. One time, James Dobson interviewed both of us after the publication of the book we wrote together, *God of My Father*.[1] I'll never forget the moment. I'm experiencing it now as I write about it.

In the middle of the interview, Dr. Dobson leaned toward Dad and, with warmth you could feel, said, "Mr. Crabb, you must be very proud of your son." I struggled to maintain my composure. My father had never put into words that he loved me or was proud of me. I waited, not sure if I was stretched out on a guillotine or about to be crowned.

Dad shifted in his chair. Then he spoke. "Well, we have to be careful not to get big heads, but yes, God has used Larry in a variety of ways."

That was it. The blade dropped. It's been hard to get my big head back in place. At that moment, I would have given anything to see Dad beam and to hear him say, "Dr. Dobson, if I had my choice of any man in history, I'd have chosen Larry for my son." I believe he could have said those words and meant them. The passion I longed to hear was in him, but he didn't enter his "red dot." Why?

Why do most of us, even the emotionally expressive among us who easily say, "I love you" and "I think the world of you," why do we so rarely speak from our depths? Why do most of us never even realize there are unexplored depths within us, let alone enter them? When our Lord spoke, people knew something about His words was radically different. What was it?

He spoke with authority. He spoke from the center of His being. He knew who He was in His core and was comfortable in being exactly who He knew Himself to be. He was the most, the only, authentic person who ever lived. He was familiar with the depths within Him, and He always spoke out of those depths in ways that suited His God-honoring purposes.

Why aren't we more authentic? What keeps us more social than real? Do we fear that if we were real, we would run from others in terror of rejection or run toward them in pathetic neediness or maybe in violent hatred? Was Freud right? Do we have to somehow keep our desires in check, while at the same time indulge enough of them to keep us reasonably happy?

Why was my father so afraid to say what was in his heart? Why do I have the same struggle? Could I learn to be more authentic, at least with God, to present myself before Him in my red dot?

It's important that I do. And it's important for you as well. Without presenting ourselves to God, without entering our red dot and speaking authentically from whatever is there, we will never develop the relationship with Him that we long for, that He longs for, that we could enjoy together.

What keeps us from getting real with God? Let me address that question first. The other question, how to get real, I'll respond to next.

OUR DEEPEST LONGING AND OUR WORST TERROR

Most of us live life on its surface. We may think we've gone beneath, especially when we've suffered or risked big or told our story to our small group.

But we've not reached our center until we've faced and felt a longing that nothing in this world can satisfy. More than anything else, we yearn to be in a relationship where the love we receive defines our identity and the meaning we live for defines our value, where we can then live as the unique people we are, following the unique calling on our lives.

Because we intuitively sense that something about us is difficult to accept, something worse than what we do, something terrible that defines who we are, we intuitively sense our need to relate with someone who can forgive us and envision who we could become.

That desire is shared by men and women. Men feel the whisper of a call to move out and take hold of their worlds, to move into others with weight that is felt and respected. Nothing terrifies a man more than to think his life amounts to nothing more than a hand dipped into water and then withdrawn, with no evidence that it was ever there.

A man's fear is this: *Am I adequate? Do I have the weight to handle important tasks, to impact a woman, a child, a friend, in a way that affirms my value?* The flip side of desire is terror—the coin has two sides. *I want what I can't stop wanting. Is what I want so desperately—eternal value, the weight to make an impact that lasts beyond the grave—mine to enjoy?* A man's deepest terror is weightlessness, the absence of solid substance that others recognize and appreciate.

Women are not men. Men are not women. The differences extend beyond physiology and anatomy, beyond hairstyle and clothing and pitch of voice and the way each throws a ball or moves on a dance floor or tilts the head when puzzled. The core difference lies in desire. Men long for weightiness, for the substance that impacts.

Women yearn for beauty, for an internal reality that makes eternal impact by drawing others to cherish and honor and protect what they see, by awakening in others their desire for ultimate beauty. Nothing terrifies a woman more than to feel that there is nothing unique about her being that another could esteem and treasure.

A woman's fear is this: *Am I beautiful, or am I merely useful? A sexual object? A resource that functions well to achieve another's purpose?* The flip side of desire is terror. *Can I connect deeply with anyone? Is anyone safe? Will anyone see my beauty, or is there nothing to see that others will honor or enjoy?*

We're not sure. We're not sure if anybody will do for us what we need so badly but can't do for ourselves. Men feel like weightless little boys, women like invisible little girls.

With fallen ingenuity, we handle our terror by shoving our deepest longings out of awareness and assuming control over lesser ones. With terror numbed, we live to protect ourselves. We find a relational style that keeps us feeling pretty good, and when something threatens to arouse our deep pain and terror, we retreat or attack. We do whatever it takes to keep ourselves intact.

Our red dot of unsatisfied desire and consuming terror stays hidden.

Dad would have loved to know he had the weight he longed to have in my life. He lost his father when he was five. His mother (whom I knew) was more pious than affectionate, more determined to trust God with four kids, no husband, and no money than to pour her feminine beauty into her children.

I don't think Dad ever felt the depth of his value. All his life he felt inadequate. Given his internal emptiness, he was a first-class father. And I am grateful. I respect and love him.

But he did what all men do. He let his terror of weightlessness get in the way of pouring his masculine depth into my starving soul. I struggle with the same problem as a husband, dad, friend, and counselor. I struggle to present the emptiness of my unsatisfied desire and the controlling power of my consuming terror to God. So do Melanie and Stan.

"Sure," says Melanie, "I'm mad, and I'm hurt. Am I scared? You bet. Will I have to feel this miserable the rest of my life?"

Stan chimes in. "Look, all I want to know is whether I should visit my father or not. Am I hurt that he's never been there for me? Do I still feel pain when I think about it? Of course. That's why I don't think about it.

What's the point? I think I'm pretty well healed of all those wounds. I'm not drinking, and I'm there for my kids. Besides, if I really let myself feel the pain that's still in me somewhere, I think I might start crying and never stop. What's the good in that?"

My word to Melanie and Stan, and to you and to me, is this: If you never enter your red dot, you'll never discover the God whose love displaces terror. And you'll never discover the real you, the wonderful you that's strong and beautiful, weighty and desirable. You'll never find yourself until you find God in your red dot, or until He finds you in your brokenness.

How to Enter Your Red Dot

If something is stirring within you, if you can feel a desire to enter your internal world of reality and present yourself to God, then consider three suggestions.

First, make a lifestyle of reflection on your red dot. No, I'm not suggesting you get obsessed about it. Eat your lunch and call your friend and go to work without always wondering what's happening in your depths. But yes, I am suggesting that you take a break a few times every day. Spend a few minutes asking yourself, "What am I aware of going on in me right now? What am I feeling? What am I wishing would happen? What am I scared of?"

When you wake up at two in the morning, don't immediately grab a book or switch on the TV or take a pill. Lie there and reflect on what's stirring in your heart and mind. Tell God about it. Call Him Papa.

"Papa, right now I'm feeling like I'll never get above the pile. I have so much to do, and here I am, wide-awake in the middle of the night. I'm mad at You, I'm mad at life, and I'm mad at my wife for sleeping so soundly.

"But I want to keep going. I'm a guy. I want to know I can handle whatever life throws at me. I'm not sure I can. I'm not man enough to move through the pressure with courage. I'd rather find some pretty girl on TV I can lust over for a while. Or just lie here in bed and play a porn film in my mind. Or maybe get up and list what I have to get done today. Maybe I should go downstairs and read a devotional book, to get my mind on spiritual things.

"But I can use the devotional the same way I use sexual fantasies, to keep away from my red dot. OK, what is going on?"

Don't expect that a one-time effort to face where you are will strike pay dirt. Make it a lifestyle. A few minutes every day. A time every evening or early morning. Reflect on what's going on in you as you pick up your Bible or open your devotional book. Make a lifestyle of reflecting on your red dot. That's suggestion number one. It will help you know what's going on inside you when you present yourself to God.

Second, pay attention to your dreams. No, I'm not a Jungian or a Freudian, but especially vivid dreams that you clearly remember the next morning sometimes express hidden conflict you've purposefully hidden. If you're going to present more and more of yourself to God, use various opportunities (like dreams) to peek into the world of your thoughts and feelings.

Just last night, I dreamed that I was at the gym, bench-pressing a weight I normally handle easily, when my arms went limp and the barbell crashed into my chest, broke my ribcage, and I was rushed by ambulance to the hospital. I remember feeling relieved, almost giddy, that I would be taken care of.

I thought about my dream this morning. A heavy speaking schedule is on the horizon, dozens of e-mails await my response, a desire to enjoy my family gnaws at me, and a couple of big deadlines are closing in. I've handled similar seasons of pressure for forty years.

But as I visualized the barbell falling and my arms having no power to resist the impact, I could feel the terror that maybe this time I'd be exposed as an imposter. I'm not a man. I'm a little boy. I have no strength. All these years I've been pretending. I can't handle all that's on my plate. Why pretend? Maybe I'll just go out to breakfast, skip the oatmeal and order an omelet, read the sports page and funnies, and escape from this madness. I think that was the trip to the hospital. The dickens with manhood. Be a passive hedonist. Let someone else take care of me. There, that relieves the terror.

I awoke at four this morning. I spent half an hour talking this over with God. I presented myself, stirred by the dream. I was at my desk by five thirty, writing, eating a bowl of cereal with blueberries, and working on this chapter. It felt good. I felt alive again, sweating and moving ahead like a man, lifting heavy weights with ease.

Third, follow the "affective track" in the presence of a trusted friend. *Affect* simply means emotion. Stay on the lookout for distinct feelings that arise within you. They may be ugly emotions like perverted lust or violent anger. They may be glorious emotions such as an exhilarating sense of freedom or joy. Or they might just be everyday emotions, like impatience with rude drivers or pleasure in a good cup of coffee.

Suzanne was telling me about her unengaging father and her critical mother as if she were describing a dull movie. No affect. No emotion. Flat as a pancake.

I said, "I can't imagine you wouldn't be angry."

"Oh no, I've dealt with all that."

"That's certainly possible. But I would think if you had, you'd be telling me your story with real disappointment and with the warmth of having forgiven them. I suspect you're still really mad at them."

"I don't think so," she insisted, "but I'll reflect on what you said."

The next day, she said, "For the first time in my life, I stomped around my bedroom yelling and screaming. I can't believe how much anger I had toward my father. My husband was there, listening to the whole thing. And he held me when I let him; he didn't try to stop me from yelling. He was just there. And this morning I'm more aware of God's love for me than I've ever been. I let Him see me at my worst, and I knew He still loved me. It's wonderful."

Tune in. Meditate on what you feel. See your affect as a doorway opening in front of you. Walk through it. See where it leads. Don't analyze. Don't try to see what your emotions mean or where they come from. Simply flow with them. Follow their lead.

Talk out loud about your affective red dot with a friend. Getting real with a trusted friend will make it easier to get real with God, and to feel His love.

A Personal Example

One more example, this one brief and personal. Yesterday, the pressure of all that lies ahead got to me. I panicked. I lost perspective. But I didn't try to calm myself down or recite Bible verses to gain perspective.

I asked my wife if she had a few minutes. She said yes. I told her I was an emotional basket case. I ranted and raved for maybe ten minutes, paying attention to what was happening in my chaotic inner world.

I noticed that an urge to pray appeared. I felt foolish. Was this just a religious veneer, a weightless ritual that Rachael would politely endure but know was only a performance?

I told God I was scared. I presented myself to Him. Then I mustered up my courage and said to my wife, "I want to pray." And I did. She smiled. I smiled back. I went back to my work with a new trace of hope. "Yes, I'm here. No pressure can destroy me. Time to move on."

Present yourself to God. He'll present Himself to you. That's the first *P* in the PAPA prayer.

Before you move on to the next letter in the PAPA prayer, you might find it a useful exercise to reflect on how Melanie and Stan could present themselves to God. Use your imagination.

ATTEND TO
HOW YOU ARE THINKING OF
GOD

chapter fourteen

❧

Who Do You Think You're Talking To?

*W*hat picture of God comes to mind when you pray? Who do you assume He is? What's He like?

Notice I'm not asking what picture or idea you consciously choose and then try to keep in your mind, but what conception of God is already in you that, perhaps beneath your awareness, rumbles around when you talk to Him?

The second step in learning the PAPA prayer is to attend to who you think you're talking to when you pray and then to correct whatever misrepresentation becomes clear. As you work through this step, you may realize you have no idea who God is. No picture emerges. No image comes to mind.

That might be a good thing. Sometimes we pray most meaningfully when we have no sense that He is present, or even exists. It's then that deliberate faith, a strong act of the will, carries our prayers. Life can get so dark that we must draw on the kind of faith that stubbornly continues to hang on to what we once knew was true.

The richest prayers often arise out of an emotionally empty heart. Let me comment on that idea for a minute.

When You Have No Picture of God

In C. S. Lewis's fascinating book *The Screwtape Letters*, senior demon Screwtape is counseling his protégé Wormwood on the ways of the "Enemy," who from hell's perspective, of course, is God. He says, "You must have often wondered why the Enemy does not make more use of His power to be sensibly present to human souls in any degree He chooses and at any moment. Merely to override a human will (as His felt presence in any but the faintest and most mitigated degree would certainly do) would be for Him useless. He cannot ravish. He can only woo."[1]

That's a thought worth some reflection. Screwtape continues, "He will set them off with communication of His presence which, though faint, seems great to them, with emotional sweetness, and easy conquest over temptation."

Many of us have had moments when we were overwhelmed by an unmistakable sense of God's presence, and, in those moments, lifting Him to first place in our affections seemed natural. Have you ever wondered why the Spirit doesn't extend those moments through the rest of our lives? Screwtape knows.

"But He never allows this state of affairs to last long. Sooner or later He withdraws, if not in fact, at least from his conscious experience. . . . He leaves the creature to stand up on its own legs—to carry out from the will alone duties which have lost all relish."

Don't miss Screwtape's "wisdom." I would put it this way: *we are never more fully who we really are than when we follow God whether we experience Him or not.* Faith that believes when it cannot see releases our true identity; it weakens both the defenses that blur that identity and the self-serving passions that too often rule our choices.

"It is during such tough periods," Screwtape goes on, "that it [the human being assigned to Wormwood's care] is growing into the sort of creature He wants it to be. Hence the prayers offered in the state of dryness are those which please Him most."

So don't worry if no picture of God or clear idea of who He is comes to mind when you pray. You may be in a place that leads into the richest communion with God. That, of course, troubled Screwtape. Listen to one last comment.

"Do not be deceived, Wormwood. Our cause is never more in danger than when a human, no longer desiring, but still intending to do our Enemy's will, looks round upon a universe from which every trace of Him seems to have vanished, and asks why he has been forsaken, and still obeys." I would add, and still prays—not to an unknown God, but to an unfelt God.

If you attend to God and sense only the darkness of a cave, you are perhaps in the best school for learning the PAPA prayer.

WHEN YOU HAVE A FALSE PICTURE OF GOD

Most of us, however, most of the time, if we pay deliberate attention to the picture of God that without effort forms in our mind when we pray, see something. Some idea of God is fixed in our minds that comes less from a direct revelation of God and more from early encounters with church and our earthly dads.

I asked one person who she visualized God to be as she talked to Him, and she quickly replied, "A pygmy in a wheelchair." I hadn't heard that one before, so I asked what that strange image symbolized. "I sometimes feel like I'm talking to an undersized person who's too disabled, though He means well, to do much of anything."

Another said, "I really hadn't paid attention to it before, but I think I picture God as an angry white-haired man with a flowing robe, outstretched arms, and fire coming out of His eyes, the kind of person you'd be most likely to meet in a nightmare."

I read her John's description of Jesus in the first chapter of Revelation. She said, "That's Him!" I suspect the painting of Moses throwing down the tablets of stone in a rage shaped her image as well.

A friend who has prayed two years for a job that hasn't come said, "When I pray, all I see is a blank stare."

No one I spoke with described God as a Santa Claus figure, but I suspect that has more to do with "religious correctness" than honesty. How else are we supposed to imagine God when a television preacher warmly exhorts us, "Declare God's favor and get ready for blessings. He loves to shower His children with good things. Believe God when things are hard, and they will get better. He'll give you the new house you want, the better job, a boss who is more supportive. That's what He loves to do."

Believe that message, and you'll picture God in a red suit on a sleigh loaded with goodies on His way to your house.

How do you picture God when you pray? Whatever idea of God is in your mind as you talk with Him will influence the way you pray. It's possible that millions of Christians across the world who think they're praying in Jesus's name are in fact praying in the name of someone else, to a God that the Bible knows nothing of.

TEN COMMON IMAGES OF GOD

I've identified ten common images of God that are in people's minds when they pray. See if one (or a blend of several) of these describes the God you pray to:

1. Smiling Buddy
2. Backroom Watchmaker
3. Preoccupied King
4. Vending Machine
5. Stern Patriarch

6. Kindly Grandfather
7. Impersonal Force
8. Cruel Tyrant
9. Moral Crusader
10. Romantic Lover

The Bible won't let us pin God down to one image that we can get comfortable with. The God we meet from Genesis to Revelation, including the God we see up close in the four Gospels, is hard to classify. The more we read, the deeper the mystery becomes. He is at once endearing, furious, sensitive, aloof, playful, holy, welcoming, terrifying, responsive, and unpredictable—not the sort of God we easily call Papa.

We want to pin Him down, to at least know who it is we're dealing with, good or bad. We like to say things such as, "Whenever He closes one door, He opens another," especially when we've just lost a job. Or, "This trial has come into my life to teach me a lesson." That view of God, as teacher, lets us hope that if we learn the lesson quickly, we'll be out on the playground soon.

One more thing we like to say about God: "He's always there when I need Him." A reliable God is a source of comfort, like a teddy bear. We want to believe that no dark night has to feel like a dark night.

We want to know who it is we're talking to when we pray. We hate mystery. And we want to be able to count on Him to do what we expect. We like control, or at least predictability. So we come up with images of God that emerge from our early experiences with church and fathers, and that serve our purposes. Here are brief descriptions of those ten images.

1. SMILING BUDDY

In the film *Wide Awake,* Rosie O'Donnell, as a baseball-cap-wearing nun, had her students read *Jesus Is My Buddy* as a homework assignment. He's there for you the way a good friend should be. Immanence without transcendence, with us but not above us—a God who just likes hanging out. No demands. No rules. Just a good time.

Think of God as a smiling buddy, and prayer will become nothing more than asking favors from a chum.

2. BACKROOM WATCHMAKER

This is the way I most often misperceive God. At times, I'm a functional deist. I sometimes feel alone in an indifferent universe, designed and wound up to keep ticking by a craftsman who never leaves the shop. He made the clock. Now He has other things to do. I prayed for my brother's safe flight the day his plane crashed and killed him. *Que sera, sera.* Whatever will be, will be. Why bother with prayer? The clock keeps ticking.

This picture of God for years kept my prayers dull and lifeless, the product of a resigned attitude that tried to accept whatever happened as somehow good.

3. PREOCCUPIED KING

Despite assurances that no sparrow falls to the ground without God knowing, we sometimes picture God as preoccupied with more important matters than what school we choose for our kids or whether to visit a dying father we don't like. He's absorbed with evangelism, crusades, political battles over abortion, and which church plant will become the next megachurch.

Our prayers feel small, petty, not worthy of our preoccupied king's attention. But we pray anyhow, the way a small-town grocer writes to his congressman about business regulations that will force him to close down.

4. VENDING MACHINE

The most common image of God that we don't admit to but still hold is akin to Santa Claus or to a smiling buddy, with this difference: you don't have to relate to a vending machine. Just put in the coins and collect your treat. I wonder how much of our worship and declarations of love for God express the same sentiment felt by a satisfied consumer walking away from a vending machine, biting into his Snickers candy bar.

We pray right. It works. The parking spot opened up. The lump disappeared. The new job came along. Let's pray more. Let's insert more coins. God is good.

5. STERN PATRIARCH

This one often develops out of experience with religious fathers or legalistic churches. Carry the biggest Bible you can find to school. Walk away when someone uses a bad word. Place your napkin on your lap when you sit for dinner and wait quietly till Father arrives. Take a bite before he blesses the food, and you'll be sent to your room without eating.

With this picture in our minds, God can be obeyed but not enjoyed. The idea of dancing with the Trinity (a favorite of mine) is near blasphemous, at least ridiculous. Prayer is stiff, rigid, the result of transcendence (God above us) without immanence (God with us). Worship lacks passion. Petitions are offered in a shy voice.

6. KINDLY GRANDFATHER

One of my favorite things to do is sit with my grandkids in front of the fireplace. They snuggle, they laugh, and they tease one another and me. It's fun. But when their teasing crosses a line and I call a halt, they sometimes seem surprised. That's what parents do, not grandparents. Our job is to let them skip vegetables and go right to the ice cream.

Prayers to a kindly grandfather sound like the whiny pleadings of an insufferably adorable child. A little girl hugs your neck. A little boy playfully pokes your arm. "OK, you can have candy before dinner. But just one piece. Well, maybe two."

7. IMPERSONAL FORCE

This is the "blank stare" image of God. Not the watchmaker who has already done what he's going to do. Not the king who's preoccupied with concerns more important than yours. Watchmakers and kings at least are people who can be persuaded. But this idea of God is a power that cannot be harnessed. It's the image of an impersonal force. Straight from *Star Wars*.

We don't respond with the fatalism of a deist. We feel more the despair of an impotent person in a world of uncontrollable power. If God wants us to have cancer, we'll get cancer. We'll pray for healing, but with no excitement, no real hope. Nothing we do makes a difference. God is more a thing than a person. Prayer, at best, might redirect the flow of electricity, but it never connects you to someone who loves you. There is no relationality in this view.

8. CRUEL TYRANT

It's hard at times to not see God as cruel. He directed Satan's attention to Job, a good man, and then turned the devil loose to torture him. It sometimes takes real effort to call God good. And when you doubt His goodness, sin seems eminently reasonable. Why not? Find a little pleasure in a world run by a God who has no interest in looking out for you. Is that so wrong?

Prayer? Pray (to whom is unclear) that the cruel tyrant will have a change of heart. Or try to believe He's good deep down and needs a little coaxing to display His better side.

9. MORAL CRUSADER

In this one, what God hates most are visible sins, the sins of culture—abortion, pornography, gambling, same-sex marriage, racism, political corruption (defined by some circles as closely joined to liberalism), and adultery, to name a few. Personal spiritual formation is a secondary concern. Turning the national tide back to God is the first thing. That needs to be the passion of our prayers, at all-night vigils, prayer conferences, and stadium events.

Mobilize resources and raise money. Make something happen. Devote your best spiritual energy to praying about the things that matter most to the moral crusader we worship.

(An image similar to moral crusader is theological stickler. It's common among nonrelational theologians, pharisaical elders, and controlling pastors. Prayers to a theological stickler involve smugly joining forces with God to persuade people of one's firm views on matters such as eschatology and mode of baptism and church structure with little or no concern for what's going on in people's hearts, whether they relate to God and others in a way that draws people to the gospel. Church leaders who pray to a theological stickler use good phrases like "We need to preach the Word" as a smokescreen to keep their own internal garbage and self-serving relational lifestyle out of sight. I mention this one in parentheses because, in today's culture, we're more aware that doctrine is vital not for its own sake but for its impact on how we live.)

10. ROMANTIC LOVER

God loves us, as individuals. What else needs to be said? What else matters? He longs to satisfy our hearts, to communicate how profoundly He loves us so that we can feel valuable, special, and cherished. Center your life on pursuing the experience of deep connection to God. Pray for it. Whatever comes into your life that provides an experience of ecstasy, of soul connection, thank God for it. Whatever creates misery, run from it, into the arms of your Lover.

With this understanding of God, prayer is reduced to the narcissistic yearnings of the self-worshiper, one who values the experience of internal satisfaction now above all other goods.

There they are. Ten pictures of God that come to our minds when we pray. Each one distorts prayer into something other than relating to the God who is who He is.

How do you picture God when you pray? Think about it. Attend to it. Next time you talk to God, step back for a minute and ask yourself, "Who do I think I'm talking to?"

Then ask a very different question: "Who is He? Do I even know?" We'll consider that in the next chapter.

chapter fifteen

⟳

Who Has God Shown Himself to Be?

In Hebrews 1:3, we're told that Jesus is the "exact representation" of His Father. So if we want to know who the Father is, what He's like, we can look at Jesus. We're supposed to. The visible Son is a mirror image of the invisible Father. One great advantage of the incarnation (God in human form) is that now we can see God. Just look at Jesus.

In this chapter, we're going to do exactly that—we're going to take a close look at Jesus as He is right now, in order to get a clear picture of God, of the Papa we're talking to when we pray.

Praying to God is something like e-mailing a relative you've never met, who lives in a place you've never been. In return correspondence (to embellish the analogy), your relative never sends a picture of himself, never sends a picture of his house or land, and always writes a generic letter addressed to "My much loved relatives," like the ones we receive every Christmas. His e-mails never come only to you and are therefore never addressed only to you. He never calls. And you can't call him. He has no phone.

It would be nearly impossible to not imagine what this person we've never seen looks like. Is he tall? Skinny? Nice-looking? Is the country where he lives dry and flat or green and rolling? And how about his home? Ranch style? Modern? Tudor?

He never tells us. We ask. He never replies. Just like God. So we give up all hope of forming a clear picture of what our relative looks like or where he lives.

We become aware, however, that what we really want is to know him. Whether he is clean-shaven or bearded doesn't matter. What's he like? What would he be like to be with? Now that we've moved past the surface stuff, we're curious about what matters.

Maybe that's why the Bible tells us so little of the kinds of things we usually want to know about someone we've never met. We're intended to move past the social matters to the personal. Who is this God we pray to?

Who Is God?

I'm not sure if, until recently, I've ever asked personal questions about God, if I've ever thought hard about who He is and how it would feel to be with Him. I think I've assumed I already knew. After all, I was raised on picture storybooks about God. I've seen flannel-graph cutouts, stuck on a blue background, of Jesus sitting on the rim of a well, talking to a lonely lady. I know dozens of hymns by heart that talk about God from every conceivable angle.

I've seen Jesus in Mel Gibson's movie. I've watched Charlton Heston's Moses disappear into a cloud to meet with God. I've been glued to the screen as C. S. Lewis (played by Anthony Hopkins) peered through the thick fog of earth's Shadowlands to catch a glimpse of what lay beyond.

But I'm not sure I've ever seriously wondered who God is, right now, in this exact moment. Without troubling my head about it, I've assumed God was the cosmic craftsman, the backroom watchmaker who made the world, set its gears in place, and then let it tick away. At other times, I've preferred to see Him as my romantic lover whom I have every right to expect will satisfy me.

It occurs to me that I may have had my clearest, most accurate glimpses of God when He was most obscure, most mysterious, and uncategorizable. My father loved to say that real spiritual maturity meant to enjoy God's delightful unpredictability. Hmm. Worth pondering.

I've never expected to literally see God, ever. Perhaps in heaven Papa will somehow be visible to us, but I doubt it. I know I'll see Jesus, and I think then I'll understand His words, "Anyone who has seen me has seen the Father" (John 14:9). I'll be content with that. Fully satisfied. Delirious.

But what about now? I don't see Papa. I don't see Jesus. I don't see the Spirit. What picture, if any, am I to form of Papa when I talk to Him?

Like our e-mailing relative, God doesn't send a photo album replete with snapshots of Him talking to Abraham or of Jesus driving out vendors from the temple. But He does something better. He has compiled a collection of pictures-in-narrative, none that reduce Him to one comfortable image but a scrapbook filled with stories. Some of them disturb us, but when we enter them deeply enough, they powerfully draw us toward Him.

At the end of this scrapbook of stories, He includes a final few pages of images. Images reach deeper than stories, certainly deeper than didactic teaching. When the Spirit wanted to finish the Bible, He wrote Revelation, the unveiling of Jesus Christ through images.

One author writes, "No other book helps us see Jesus *as he is right now* as clearly and compellingly as the last book John wrote."[1] I would add that no other book as clearly and compellingly creates an image of God that we can—and should—picture when we pray. We'll never see our Papa, but we can see Him in Jesus.

Look with me, first at the context of the first image of Jesus that John saw, then at the image itself. And as you read the next few pages, attend to God. Is the image that's presented different from the way you've pictured God?

A VISION OF THE RISEN CHRIST

John, the writer of Revelation, an old man in his mideighties, had been exiled to the prison camp of Patmos for treason. He had refused to drop a pinch of incense before an image of Domitian to honor the Roman emperor as *Domine et Deus* (Lord and God), and he was therefore viewed as both an atheist and an enemy of the state. John was left to die on the island of Patmos.

I would have complained. John worshiped. He had first things and second things in their proper place. Here's how he greeted his friends in a letter: "I, John, your brother and companion in the suffering and kingdom and patient endurance that are ours in Jesus, was on the island of Patmos because of the word of God and the testimony of Jesus" (Revelation 1:9).

I think I might have mentioned that my suffering was more than theirs and that my need for patient endurance was far greater than theirs.

I would have complained. John worshiped. "On the Lord's Day, I was in the Spirit," he said, looking not at his circumstances but at his Lord (v. 10).

And then it happened. Jesus Christ appeared to him. Remember, John was the one who sixty years earlier, over dinner, had rested his head comfortably on Jesus's chest. According to the custom of the day, he had "snuggled" with Jesus, masculine style.

Not long afterward, John watched Jesus writhe in agony on the cross. When he later pastored the church at Ephesus, he brought Mary, the mother of Jesus, with him to the fellowship, looking after her as Jesus had requested. He had last seen Jesus, still in the form of an ordinary man, after His resurrection, talking with John and his friends, and then lifting off the ground and floating into the clouds and out of their sight.

Had you asked John who he visualized when he prayed, I suppose it would have been one of those images. Any one would have been wonderful. But after the vision he received on Patmos, his image of Christ was never the same. It couldn't have been. Listen to his description of what he actually saw:

I heard behind me a loud voice like a trumpet. . . . I turned around to see the voice that was speaking to me. And when I turned I saw seven golden lampstands, and among the lampstands was someone "like a son of man," dressed in a robe reaching down to his feet and with a golden sash around his chest.

His head and hair were white like wool, as white as snow, and his eyes were like blazing fire. His feet were like bronze glowing in a furnace, and his voice was like the sound of rushing waters. In his right hand he held seven stars, and out of his mouth came a sharp double-edged sword. His face was like the sun shining in all its brilliance.

When I saw him, I fell at his feet as though dead. Then he placed his right hand on me and said: "Do not be afraid. I am the First and the Last. I am the Living One; I was dead, and behold I am alive for ever and ever! And I hold the keys of death and Hades." (Revelation 1:10–18)

John had seen the transfigured Christ, but he had never seen anything like this. No doubt he had sensed God's presence on Patmos many times. But now his Papa gave John a vision of Jesus Christ as He was then and is today.

Reread the description. Then move on as I simply and succinctly suggest some of what must have come to John's mind and stirred in his heart when he met Jesus Christ as he had never met Him before. My guess is that his prayers to Papa, at the end of his life, were exquisitely rich.

"I heard behind me a voice like a trumpet." Perhaps John's mind went to the apostle Paul's words, that the Lord's second coming would be announced by a trumpet (1 Thessalonians 4:16). John must have thought, "Something big is happening. Someone huge is coming."

"I turned . . . I saw . . . someone 'like a son of man.'" Hundreds of years before, Daniel had been given a vision of "one like a son of man. . . . He approached the Ancient of Days" (Daniel 7:13). The term "son of man"

refers to the most important person in all history. In the ancient Near East, it was perhaps the most pretentious title anyone could have used. In other words, John is saying, "So, it's Him! It's Jesus Christ I am seeing. No one matters more in all the universe or here on Patmos."

"Dressed in a robe reaching down to His feet and with a golden sash around his chest." The robe of a priest was on Jesus, and the sash was around his chest. When a man was preparing to work, he fastened the sash around his waist, so the flowing material wouldn't get in his way. When his work was finished, he lifted the sash around his chest.

Jesus is our priest, our bridge between man and God, the highway into Papa's presence. The sash is around His chest. The work is done. We can now stride boldly into the throne room of heaven. It's where we belong. John is telling us, "I heard Him say, 'It is finished.' It's true. Even on Patmos, I can come to God and enjoy communion with Him. Thank You, Jesus."

"His head and hair were white like wool, as white as snow." John no doubt flipped through the pages of his mind to Isaiah 1:18: "Though your sins are like scarlet, they shall be as white as snow; though they are red as crimson, they shall be like wool." Jesus Christ is ageless, wise beyond all the elders, and utterly pure. And John was seeing Him. That meant death, unless by some miracle John, too, had been declared pure, clean, undefiled.

John is saying, "I am standing in His holy presence. What more could I want? With Him, I am forever alive, and will share in the wisdom of the ages."

"And his eyes were like blazing fire." Nothing changes the human heart so deeply as to look bad in the presence of love, to be seen with all that is wickedly ugly about us and still be wanted, more, to be delighted in. That's grace.

We live to pretend, to hide what is bad and parade what is good. It prevents community from becoming grace-based and real. And it keeps us from enjoying God. But John tells us, "He sees me. He sees everything. My sin is still with me. But He remains! Can it be?"

"His feet were like bronze glowing in a furnace." Again, John's mind turned back, this time to Daniel. Nebuchadnezzar's image of human-built kingdoms consisted of a head of gold, a chest of silver, thighs of bronze, and feet of iron mixed with clay. The feet couldn't bear the weight of what humans constructed. Our self-obsession eventually destroys all community, all civilization.

But Jesus's feet were fire-tested bronze. With all its flaws, the church will never disappear. Jesus can carry our weight, all of it, from the medieval Inquisition to the last church split. John is saying, "I am your companion in the kingdom of Christ. Neither external persecution nor internal pressure can destroy my real home."

"And his voice was like the sound of rushing waters." I once stood on the sideline of an NFL football game, literally one yard from the playing field. Sixty thousand fans were screaming. The roar was so loud I had to put my mouth against my friend's ear and shout at the top of my lungs to be heard. It was exciting but unpleasant.

I have also stood at the base of Niagara Falls. The sound of rushing water is at once deafening and soothing. It blocks out all other noise and quiets my heart. As John says, "I hear nothing but Him! And my soul is at rest."

"In his right hand he held seven stars." The stars Jesus held were the angels assigned to each of the seven churches. And Jesus held them. No star is running things. Jesus is in charge. John assures us, "He is in control. I am safe from whatever would harm my soul. My body they may kill. His truth abideth still. I am secure."

"And out of his mouth came a sharp two-edged sword." The sword referred to is not the long blade of the fencer. It is rather a curved, short blade used to plunge into someone at close range.

Jesus gets up close and personal, like a surgeon. His eyes see what's wrong more clearly than the most sensitive MRI. And He cuts with a precision every surgeon would envy. John says, "Whatever is still wrong with me—and oh, it is plenty—He will cut away. It will feel like death; He uses no anesthetic. But it will make me whole."

"His face was like the sun shining in all its brilliance." One more time, John remembered his Old Testament. "The LORD bless you and keep you; the LORD make his face shine upon you and be gracious to you; the LORD turn his face toward you and give you peace" (Numbers 6:24–26). No blessing was greater to a Jew. John must have been thrilled. "He's looking at me. I feel the warmth. All is well. I am at peace."

Yet he fell at Christ's feet as though dead. When we see Jesus as He really is, today, right now, we don't casually pray, "Oh, by the way, Lord, could you arrange for a nice sunny day for my daughter's wedding?" Nor do we fervently pray with a spirit of entitlement: "Jesus, my marriage brings me such pain. Please change things so I can feel better."

Instead, we're silenced. We dare not speak till spoken to.

Then the risen Christ placed His right hand on John and spoke. "Don't be afraid. I'm alive and because I'm alive, you're alive. Advance My kingdom until I return with great power to finish the job."

THE DELIGHT OF KNOWING GOD

When John stood up after his encounter with the risen Lord, I suspect he was more fully John than ever before. Why? Knowing Papa does that to you. You become yourself by knowing Him as He really is.

No longer do we see God as a watchmaker or buddy or tyrant; now we see the transcendent God, so far above us that we can only fall down in silence before Him, saying nothing, asking nothing; and the immanent God, so fully with us that we stand up with bestowed dignity, secure, unafraid, authentic. And then, like King David, we break into a wild dance, with our Papa, and with Jesus, and with their Spirit.

Now, let me ask you to attend to your experience of God. Then change it, deliberately, consciously, every time you pray, to match the image of Revelation 1. That's step two in learning the PAPA prayer.

We've discussed what it means to present ourselves to God without pretense. We've just thought about attending to God and getting a clear, more accurate picture of who it is we're talking to.

Now, step three. Let's see what is required to come as we are (present) to God as He is (attend) and purge ourselves of whatever is blocking our relationship.

PURGE YOURSELF
OF ANYTHING THAT BLOCKS
YOUR RELATIONSHIP WITH GOD

chapter sixteen

&

Who Do You Turn to When You're Scared?

*W*hat I'm about to say is either a bunch of sweet words that have as much nourishing value as a Twinkie, or it's one of the most staggering and underappreciated truths in the Bible.

Here it is. *In the center of your soul and mine, in the exact center, the Shekhinah glory resides—the literal, real, overwhelming presence of God.* And when we live out of that center, all the self-seeking, self-serving energy that guides so much of what we think and feel and do, often without even knowing it, is miraculously displaced by love.

If that's true, then we have no choice but to admit that we don't usually live out of that center. Something's getting in the way. Some thick crust must be surrounding the center, blocking our access to it, leaving us in the control of that miserable, self-obsessed energy that we so easily mistake as necessary, even Christian.

I can think of nothing I want more than to enter the "sanctuary of the center," this holy place that is already in us where we can have communion with God. David knew about this sanctuary and what happens when we're there. "The LORD confides in those who fear him," he said in Psalm 25:14.

I long to join that conversation. I want to sit on the floor with Papa or go for a long walk with His arm resting on my shoulder and listen to Him tell me His secret thoughts, share with me His deepest feelings, and let me in on what He's doing and what He wants to do through me.

Does that sound as good to you as it does to me? I want to hear Him express His love for me in ways my earthly father never could do. And I want to be heard by Him, to know He knows all that I'm going through. I want to feel His life, His substance, stirring in me and released from me, to know that I'm neither invisible nor weightless; that I've been fully seen and am still wanted, fully wanted; that I'm being sent on a mission I've been equipped to handle, a mission that matters. I want to find myself in finding Him. I want to be released to be who I am in Christ. I want it so much I can taste it.

And it's possible. It's available to me. What I want the most I can have. For one reason: God Himself is in me.

Papa's Spirit has moved into my heart and made it His home. Every minute He's whispering that Jesus loves me, that Papa is singing over me. He's listening to the words I say and cleaning them up so they're fit to be presented to Papa.

He sees my most appalling fantasies, my most embarrassing failures, and reminds me Papa still welcomes me whenever I come to Him. And He tells me every day that I'm one of a kind, equipped as no one else in the history of time to advance His kingdom in unique ways that no one else has ever been asked to do. The Spirit in me is carrying Papa's voice into my heart, where I can hear it.

But most of us don't hear it, not always, sometimes not at all. Why not?

PURGE YOURSELF OF YOUR RELATIONAL SIN

We don't hear God's Spirit in our hearts because something's getting in the way. We have a buildup of wax in our ears that praying the PAPA prayer can clean out.

As we pour out everything in us to God (presenting), and as we more clearly see who we're talking to when we pray (attending), two things will happen. We'll become even more aware of how intensely we want to get close to God, and we'll realize how stubbornly and foolishly we resist it.

There's a third thing that will happen. We'll feel impotent and humbled. We'll realize we have no power to make this relationship with God be all that we want it to be, that any true experience of God is given, not achieved; and we'll see that our part in making ourselves available for this relationship involves our willingness to recognize and confess the obstacles we have created between ourselves and our Papa.

Here's where we run headlong into the problem of self-deception. We're blind to our worst faults. We can see what's wrong with everybody else (especially our spouse and kids and friends and pastors), but we can't see—we don't want to see—what's wrong with us.

And it's not because nothing much is wrong. It's easy for us to say, "Well, I know I make mistakes; after all, I'm no saint, but . . ." and then go on to enjoyably point out the flaws in others.

Something is wrong with us, and it's serious. And what is most wrong with us, what we have the hardest time seeing, shows up in the way we relate. Let me illustrate.

I was talking with two committed Christian people—sincere, kind, lovely people, married for thirty-plus years in a solid relationship. Each reports feeling loved by the other, and both are active in their church, involved with their kids and grandkids, and currently coteaching a Sunday school class on marriage.

There's just one problem. It's why they were talking with me. Gail is a nervous wreck. Behind the scenes, hidden from view, she worries if she's a good enough grandma, if her dinner guests are enjoying themselves, if the Sunday school class is being well received.

After two conversations, I invited her husband to join us. Why? I believe that everything wrong is somehow related to what's wrong in our primary relationships.

I asked him, in so many words, to share his red dot. Tom eagerly jumped into an animated discussion of the possibility of accepting a position as executive pastor of their large and still growing church. More than twenty years in the insurance business had worn him out.

When Tom took a breath, Gail muttered, "I think it's a great idea. It'll be a cut in pay, and maybe longer hours. And I guess things like that scare me a little, but Tom is really excited about it."

As she spoke, Tom turned his head slightly in her direction. Then, as soon as she finished, he turned back to me. "I know there'll be a few bumps. But the more I pray about it, the more convinced I am God is in this. You see, I've felt a passion for ministry for years, and . . ."

While Tom went on, I noticed that Gail's gaze drifted downward, she fiddled with her hands, and she looked flat. No sparkle in her expression matched his.

So I interrupted Tom and asked, "Gail, what's going on in you right now?"

"Well, I am a little uncertain. I know it means a lot to Tom, so I'm supportive, but—"

Tom interrupted. "And I'm really appreciative of Gail's support. I think she'll have more opportunities to minister, maybe together with me. I really am excited. I just want people to know Jesus, to be set free by Him."

I spoke again. "Gail, I wonder if you're feeling dismissed by Tom."

Remember, now, these are good people. I'd rank their marriage in the top 20 percent of the marriages I've seen.

Gail looked at me. I thought I saw terror in her eyes. Tom's expression was as if he'd just quickly turned around in the kitchen to reach for something and hit his seven-year-old daughter in the face who he didn't even know was there.

"I do that a lot, don't I?" Tom's voice was softer, quiet, gentle.

She began to cry.

For the next hour, we talked about Tom's loneliness, how unseen he felt. At work, he was the guy who could figure out your insurance needs and come up with a cost-effective plan to meet them. At church, he taught classes, had received lay counselor training, and talked to lots of people who appreciated his time.

"But nobody knows me. My kids don't. They see me as a fun-loving guy who's always there. And Gail, well, I guess I do feel kind of known by her, but I don't know if I've ever tried to really know her. I appreciate her, I love her, we have great times together, but I don't really know her. Maybe I thought it was her job to know me, or at least to accept me and to support whatever I do."

Gail warmly put her arm through his and said, "I've felt shut out for years. Just like I felt growing up. But I've never wanted to burden you with me. I've been afraid you wouldn't listen."

Now with tears in his eyes, Tom looked at me and said, "I've failed my wife. Why didn't I see it before? I really did dismiss her a few minutes ago. I didn't want to hear what she had to say."

And that's the question: why didn't he see it before?

Relational Sin Starts with Fear

Let me suggest something disturbing. *Right now, we're all living with relational sin that we do not see.* We hurt people we love and don't even know it. We think we're touching the hearts of our spouses, but we're not. We assume our friendships are close, but we're living on different planets.

Why? What's going on? What do we need to see that praying the PAPA prayer, along with good conversation, can reveal?

It starts with fear. From the time we were little kids, we felt afraid. We'd keep the blankets tight around our necks so the vampire wouldn't bite us. We'd keep our hands tucked in next to our bodies, never dropping them over the side of the bed because, if we did, the alligator hiding beneath our bed would chew them off.

But our real fear was deeper. We were terrified we wouldn't measure up, no one would like us, we'd be alone. When you got lost on your way home from second grade, when your dad lost his temper, when your mom was late coming home, when your uncle touched you where he shouldn't have, you were afraid. *Does anyone care? Will anyone be there when I need them? Does anyone know who I am and like me? Are they strong enough to protect me? Am I alone?*

No child naturally trusts God. Trust is always a supernatural activity, a work of the Spirit.

No adult fully trusts God. Complete trust is always a possibility, but it's never a reality until heaven.

We don't grasp the staggering truth that right now, in the center of our heart, the Spirit is there. Right now, at the right hand of Papa, Jesus is praying for us. And right now, from heaven's throne, our Papa is watching over us, loving us, arranging everything for our good.

We don't really believe that, not completely. We still live too often as if we're on our own, needing to protect ourselves from vampires and alligators, from inconsiderate husbands, cold wives, sulky children, and disloyal friends.

That's relational sin. We protect ourselves from what God tells us we don't need to fear. We devote our creative energies to calm our terror, to find some way to feel alive and wanted and happy.

Neglected kids find hobbies that turn into adult careers. Success feels good. Heads turn when we walk into the business meeting or our medical office.

Loved kids figure out what keeps their parents loving them and then parade their virtues, or they don't trust their parents' love and find comfort elsewhere. As adults, they shop for a new spouse when the old one disappoints them or they become pastors, missionaries, good people who display their goodness for all to see.

We all do it, in a thousand different ways. We all find a way to calm our fears, to pass ourselves off as someone whom others will want or someone whom others might find no reason to reject.

And it seems so necessary, so justified, so right. And it's so subtle. We just don't see it. It's who we are, and it's OK. *It's him who's wrong; it's her. Not me.* The way we're relating is keeping us at least a little bit safe, if not quite happy.

Terror goes underground. Our fear that no one could see us and want us, that our lives have no real meaning, stays hidden beneath all the ways we relate that keep us feeling pretty good.

Yet, because we haven't yet discovered the sound of our Father's voice, the one voice that can calm our deepest terror, our fears continue to drive us. We remain obsessed with ourselves, and we don't see it. We're blind to our worst faults. We do not recognize relational sin in our lives.

Tom didn't see his relational sin—until the Spirit opened his eyes through a good conversation.

God often uses discerning, loving community to lead us to new levels of purging, but He always uses prayer. Relational prayer, a good conversation with our all-seeing, all-loving Papa, is essential if our purging is to run deep. Without God's wisdom and love, we'll never see our ongoing relational sin.

So how can we relationally pray in order to have our eyes opened to the freedom of seeing our sin and repenting, and then to release the life of God that's already in us to love others well?

Read on.

chapter seventeen

Abandon Yourself to Holiness

*P*ray to purge? What does that mean? How do we do it?

We're off to a good start if we agree that what most needs purging in our lives is least easily seen, and if we agree that what is most wrong with us shows up most reliably in the way we relate. Deep purging will always involve relational sin. And the deepest purging will always center on the way we treat God.

Praying to purge, to see what's most wrong with the way we relate, begins with a genuine openness to seeing what's wrong. And it continues with a confidence that beneath whatever is wrong is holy desire, a longing to love God and love others.

Let me suggest a simple way to come to God to be purged of sin and to release what's holy. Ask two questions: First, what's wrong with the way I relate? Second, what do I want most in this relationship?

Ask God those questions. Talk to your Papa about it. Tell Him you really want Him to answer you, because you really do want to clear out anything getting in the way of your relationship.

Papa knew long before I did that Tom was so consumed with feeling valuable and important that he did not love his wife well. And Tom had been praying, "Lord, show me whatever I need to see in order to be closer to You and to serve You better." He hadn't asked the two questions exactly, but it was close enough. And God chose me (1 Corinthians 1:27 says He chooses "foolish things") to speak His answer.

If you long to hear Papa's voice, if you want to keep close company with God, if you want to enjoy Him so much that you can feel an overwhelming desire to reveal what He's like by the way you relate with others, then it's time to abandon yourself to holiness.

WHAT DOES IT MEAN TO "ABANDON YOURSELF TO HOLINESS"?

Now that's a phrase I haven't used before, so it will require some defining. It's really quite simple. We're abandoning ourselves to holiness when we come to God in prayer, wanting to see where we're wrong in the way we relate more than we want someone else to admit how they're wrong in the way they relate to us.

And that includes God. We can get so mad at Him for what He's allowed in our lives that, although we probably wouldn't put it this way, we're asking Him to confess His faults and repent.

But it goes further. We're abandoning ourselves to holiness when we come to God wanting not only to see where we're wrong but also to claim the privilege of letting others experience how God relates to them by the way we relate to them.

Now let me pause for a minute to provide a biblical background for what I'm saying. Papa told us to abandon ourselves to holiness. Through Peter, He said, "Just as he who called you is holy, so be holy in all you do" (1 Peter 1:15). Then Peter draws on his knowledge of the Old Testament and adds, "For it is written, 'Be holy, because I am holy'" (v. 16). That's a quote from Leviticus 11:44. The same words are repeated in the next verse.

But what do they mean? What is God saying? If He is ordering us to work really hard at being good until we get as good as He is, we might as well quit now. Give it up. We'll never rise to that standard by trying hard to be holy.

God, of course, knows that. None of us relates perfectly. He is well aware that the greatest saints have all died flawed, that His most avid followers have further to go on their spiritual journeys than they've already come, whether they're a decade or a day away from death.[1]

So what is God telling us to do when He says, "Be holy. Be perfect. Be as good as Me"? We're already forgiven for not being holy. But how do we now get holy? *The key is to realize God doesn't command holy action without first providing holy desire.* A closer look at the passage Peter quoted from Leviticus will, I think, begin to make that clear. Listen to the words that precede each of the two commands to be holy in verses 44 and 45.

"*I am the* LORD *your God; consecrate yourselves and be holy, because I am holy*" (emphasis mine). That's verse 44.

Now verse 45. "*I am the* LORD *your God who brought you up out of Egypt to be your God; therefore, be holy, because I am holy*" (again, I've added the emphasis).

If you put these passages together—consecrate yourselves to the Lord your God who brought you up out of Egypt to be your God—its message comes into focus. We're being told to set ourselves apart to our primary relationship. To depend on no one, not even ourselves, the way we depend on God. To set our sights on actually becoming holy, a goal we know we can't reach. To give ourselves over to the holy God who wants us (and has made it possible) to share His life. We're being told to abandon ourselves to holiness, to share in the way God relates, with radical other-centeredness, with terrible sacrifice, with humble love.

BE AWARE OF RELATIONAL SIN

But we'll never come even close to God's example of love until we clearly understand that sin is relational. We may never rob a bank, tell a lie, be intentionally mean, commit adultery, or break a promise. We may faithfully attend church, study our Bibles, visit sick people, go on missionary trips to poor countries, and give a double tithe. We may be really good people in the eyes of most everyone, especially ourselves, and still be sinning.

Relational sin is a category we don't often think about, except in its obvious forms (such as adultery), and therefore never clearly see in ourselves. Let me define it: *relational sin is anything we do for the primary purpose of getting something for ourselves.* It could be closing a business deal, winning a compliment, making ourselves happier, or relieving our terror of aloneness by gaining someone's friendship or affection. We might be doing these things with our advantage centrally in mind, but we're told to do all things for the glory of God.

That means the primary thought behind everything we do is to trust Him with our deepest needs and longings, to bring Him pleasure by putting all our eggs in His basket, to fix our hope for everything we hold dear on who He is and what He is doing and what He will yet do.

Nothing blocks our relationship with God more effectively than relational sin. Do we wonder why He seems so far away? Why our hearts are so unsatisfied in Him? Why most of our praise to God has more to do with all the blessings we have than with the intimacy He offers?

It's relational sin. We need to pray the PAPA prayer, first to present ourselves to God, then to attend to who He is, and then to ask Him two questions: "Papa, I really want to see where I'm wrong in the way I relate to You and to my spouse and friends. Will You show me? And Papa, more than anything else, I know that way down deep I have a desire, a holy desire, to treat other people the way You treat me. Will You release that desire?"

THREE EXAMPLES OF PRAYER

Let me wrap up our discussion of purging by contrasting the prayers of people who recognize relational sin and those who do not. Those for whom relational sin is not a clear category may avoid obvious sins like stealing, rape, and murder, while they unwittingly indulge in the subtle sin of protecting their own interests in relationships. And they may think they're doing nothing wrong.

Three examples will make the point: a hurting wife, a distraught dad, and a depressed person. In each case, the individual presents their struggle honestly. That's a good thing.

But then I illustrate in the left-hand column what happens when attending to a holy God and purging oneself in His presence does not take place. The result is self-obsessed petitionary prayers.

In the right-hand column, I indicate the prayer of people who know they are talking to a holy God and, consequently, face their relational sin. They want to know where they are wrong. And they want to love people better. Notice that prayers in the right-hand column remain relational in nature and, unlike those in the left-hand column, do not prematurely slide toward petition.

NOT ABANDONED TO HOLINESS	ABANDONED TO HOLINESS
and therefore unaware	and therefore aware
of relational sin	of relational sin

A HURTING WIFE

God, I don't know what to do about my husband.
I feel so unheard, so unnoticed. He rarely makes
me feel cherished. I feel like I'm losing my identity.
I hate myself; I have no sense of my worth as a woman.

Please God, either change him	Oh God, I'm seeing it.
or show me how I can live with	Nothing matters more to me

him, how I can find my voice when I'm with him. God, I need to know You'll be with me, to feel Your love, to not feel so wounded and alone. Please, help me learn how to live with my husband without losing myself.

than whether I feel good about myself. I relate to my husband with no real thought of revealing Your character to him. I don't even know what that would look like. I don't know You well enough to want to reveal You to my husband. Have mercy!

A DISTRAUGHT DAD

God, my son has been using illegal drugs for two years. I'm terrified he'll ruin his life. I've tried everything—tough love, counseling, backing off. I feel like such a failure as a father.

Please God, show me what's wrong with my son so I can know what to do. I'll do anything. Anything! Just make him better. It all seems so unfair! I know dads who spend almost no time with their kids, who provide no spiritual input, and their kids are solid, growing Christians. I just don't get it. But I know You have a good plan for my family. Please, just show me how to reach my son's heart.

Oh God, as I present myself to You, I'm beginning to see what's at stake for me. I'm terrified I'll never be able to accept myself as a man until my son straightens out. It's all about me! I see it. And it's wrong. As long as that terror drives me, I'm not loving anybody—not my son, not my wife, not You. God, I've been living to enjoy my family, not for Your glory. I've been obsessed with my dreams and demanding that You fulfill them. Have mercy!

A DEPRESSED PERSON

God, I'm sliding deeper into a dark hole, I'm crying for hours every day. I never feel good or happy. I know I'm getting really negative and that my friends are tired of me being so down, but I just feel so bad.

Please God, heal my wounds. Something must be really getting to me, but I really don't know what it is. A lot is going wrong right now—my arthritis is worse, my friends rarely call, and I don't like my job. Please, guide me to the right therapist or pastor, or to a doctor who can prescribe the best medication. I don't know how much longer I can go on living like this. Please, help me feel better.

Oh God, nobody would be drawn to You because of me. I see it! By the way I'm living, I'm telling the world that You're only worth praising when things are good, and that trusting You when things are bad means only that I'm hoping things in my life will get better. Of course I want them to, and it would make me feel better if things in my life went better. But in the middle of all this, I'm not relating to You. I'm using You. Have mercy!

Three illustrations, drawn from my life and the lives of people I've worked with. I find them convicting. Purging will continue till we're home. When you purge yourself before Papa, when you abandon yourself to holiness, you think more of how you fall short of God's holy way of relating than of how others fail you or how badly you feel or how difficult your life may be. But your focus on your own failure does not make you hate yourself, not when you're relating to your Papa. It makes you hate your sin, not yourself.

And that focus doesn't leave you discouraged and feeling heavy. Broken, yes. Despairing, no. You know that purging lights up the path of holiness, the road paved by grace that leads into God's presence, into Papa's lap. The rhythm that carries you from presenting to attending through purging carries you toward approaching God, to walking right up to God in order to enjoy the relationship with the Father you've always wanted.

APPROACH GOD
AS THE "FIRST THING"
IN YOUR LIFE

chapter eighteen

ℭℛ

You Will Hear God's Voice

$\mathcal{N}$ow we're ready. Everything so far has been prelude and preparation. We are ready to approach God. Our first three steps—presenting, attending, and purging—free us to now boldly enter into our Father's presence and tell Him that we really do want to experience Him as our greatest good, as the unrivaled "first thing" in our lives who by the sheer weight of His goodness reduces every other good thing to "second-thing" status. Approaching God completes our new paradigm for praying, the primary purpose of which is to provide a unique opportunity to get to know Him better.

But I want to be careful. I want to be sure we are on the same page when I talk about "knowing God." So let me ask you a tough question. Do you know God? Here's an even tougher one. What does it mean to know, to really know God?

Let me list a few phrases we hear a lot in Christian circles: knowing God, relating personally to God, enjoying God, loving God. What do people mean when they say those words? "I'm so grateful that I know God; I don't know how I'd live if I didn't." "I used to be a religious person, but now I have a personal relationship with God." "I enjoy being with God in ways I never dreamed were possible until I met Him."

"I love God so much. He means everything to me." Are these just words, or do they point to something real?

How Do We Relate to God?

Last night, Rachael and I spent a delightful evening with John and Phyllis and their two wonderfully maturing kids. I've known John for more than thirty years. I've known God for fifty-two. Am I using the word *known* in the same way?

We related to John's family, and we enjoyed them. And I especially enjoyed the chocolate silk pie Phyllis served for dessert.

Do I relate to God? Do I enjoy Him? When I tell you I relate to God and enjoy Him, do I mean something different than when I speak of relating to and enjoying friends? To push the point further, are there any similarities at all between enjoying God and enjoying chocolate pie?

It's not a silly point. If I really do get more enjoyment out of pie than God, then an unhealthy addiction is inevitable. Whatever brings me the most joy will prove irresistible. That's just the way we're built. We were designed to enjoy joy. When nothing brings me joy, I experience despair. When something brings me joy, I go after it. That makes it important to know what is the source of real joy, joy that's deep and lasting, without bad side effects that show up years later.

How about love? I have a pretty good idea what I mean when I say that I love my wife. But when I say that I love God, do I mean the same thing? Or is it different? And if it's different, do I mean something less or more, not as good or even better, when I say that I love Rachael?

I can see my wife, literally, with my physical eyes. I can hear her voice. I know she hears mine (and most often likes it when she does) by the expression on her face as she listens and the tilt of her head when I speak and the tone of her voice when she responds.

I touch her. She touches me. The obvious truth is that I experience my love for her in ways I can see, hear, and feel.

With God, it's different. I've never seen Him. I've read lots about Him, but I've never so much as seen a picture of Him, at least not one I knew was a close resemblance. I've never physically touched Him, and He's never physically touched me. I've never heard His audible voice (though I've come close, and a few people I trust tell me they have). And I have to believe, by faith, that He listens when I speak. I have no immediate evidence.

One measure of our love for God is whether we obey Him. But I don't love other people by obeying them. I may do what they want (for example, I took dance lessons with Rachael), but I don't think of it as obedience. It makes me wonder—is my love for God more like driving the speed limit when I spot a cop behind me? I don't like the thought.

It seems necessary to conclude that loving God is somehow different than loving my wife or kids or friends. Loving people I experience with my five senses is not the same as loving God. It can seem less real. Relating to someone I can't see sometimes doesn't seem real at all.

But it is. Knowing God, relating to Him, enjoying Him, and loving Him is real, more real than relating to anyone else. Praying the PAPA prayer, especially approaching God, is helping me believe that. It is helping me to experience the reality of my relationship with God. But how?

DISCOVER THE SOUND OF GOD'S VOICE

When you learn to pray the PAPA prayer, you will discover the sound of your Father's voice. I'm not claiming, of course, that by praying the PAPA prayer you'll one day hear a rich, Charlton Heston–like baritone voice and know it's God's. You might, but I'm making no promises. At least not that one.

I am promising that Papa will speak to you. He loves a good conversation with His children. But we have to think carefully about how He speaks to us and how we speak to Him.

Mark and Cindy have no job. Four months ago, after sixteen years in the pulpit, Mark was asked by his elders to step down as senior pastor. "We want a pastor with a clear vision for where this church is headed. You used to lead us toward measurable goals with doable strategies. Something's changed. And we don't like it. All you talk about now is knowing God better, listening for His voice, and enjoying Him more. That's too vague. We want action plans that move us toward something we can see. We want a new pastor."

Mark and Cindy were devastated. "What is church all about?" they asked. "Making something happen or knowing God better?" For the last few months, they've been waiting on God. That's what they told me.

"For what?" I asked.

"To hear from Him."

Will it happen? How will they know when it does? What will He say? How will they hear?

I remember Ellen, a lonely client who came to me when I was in practice as a psychologist. She told me that God had spoken to her through a coded message in a television preacher's sermon, inviting her to move to that preacher's city, to live with his family, and join him in ministry. Ellen had no doubt she heard from God. I had no doubt she was psychotic.

Is everyone who claims to hear from God a little off, perhaps with chemical imbalance in their brains? Or does our Papa really speak, and can we really hear Him? Does He communicate with us in ways that make it possible for us to say we know Him and relate to Him and enjoy Him and love Him without realistic risk of being labeled psychotic?

My answer (and this won't surprise you at this point in this book) is yes. What might surprise you is that my strong, loud yes is a conditional yes. Even more surprising, perhaps, is the condition. *I do not believe that we hear Papa's voice until we discover an empty, desolate void within us that is teeming with passionate desires for fullness.* Until we cut through all the legitimate happiness and pleasure in our lives, until we look beneath every sorrow and heartache that comes from living in this world, and until we enter the deepest space in our hearts that is painfully, horribly empty, we will not discover the beautiful sound of our Father's voice. At least not as clearly as we want to.

Let me tell you why I believe that. As I've said, it isn't only nature that abhors a vacuum. God does too. But the vacuum He abhors is spiritual. He can see a dry riverbed and not fill it. But He cannot see an empty heart and walk away. His love won't let Him.

COME TO GOD WITH AN EMPTY HEART

So the key to experiencing God is to come to Him with an empty heart. That means we'll need to get rid of everything we've already piled into the inner void that we hoped would fill it up. It's good to enjoy great kids and a beautiful sunset and an exciting vacation. It's right to feel pleasure in powerful ministry and an intimate marriage and a meaningful job.

But if all those good things (what I call "second things") have found their way into the center of our hearts, if we're using them to fill up that empty space reserved by God, for God, then we'll not hear His voice. Our claim to know Him and love Him will be shallow. We might try to convince ourselves our relationship with God is deep and real, but in our quiet moments, in our times of trouble, we'll know otherwise.

The key, I repeat, is to empty our inner space of everything but God and then to approach Him with freely acknowledged emptiness, claiming no hope of fullness unless He fills us. That's what it means to approach God.

It's hard to do, for at least two reasons. First, our pride gets in the way. I'm strangely offended by having to admit I need someone else to fill me up. It goes against my American individualism. And second, it terrifies me. Counterfeit fullness feels pretty good. Why give up what I already have for something I'm not sure I'll get? That's scary. It requires faith. It's easier to live by sight, by self-management, by depending on things I can see, and to some degree control, as my "first things."

But they never fill me up, not completely. It may seem like they do, but it's counterfeit fullness. If you're longing for more than a sensitive spouse or straightened-out kids or success in business, if you're aware that your only hope of real fullness is a relationship with God, then you're ready to go all the way with relational prayer.

It works like this. You'll approach God with an empty heart if you've first presented yourself to God as you really are, then attended to how you naturally think of God and corrected your wrong image according to how the Bible reveals God, and then purged yourself of everything you've come to realize is getting between you and God. The first three parts of the PAPA prayer get you ready for this last one by helping you discover how empty you are without knowing Papa well.

Honestly, ruthlessly, and continuously present, attend, and purge yourself in relational prayer; and I guarantee that you'll emerge from the process, again and again, feeling desperately empty. And that's good. That's your opportunity to develop a real relationship with God. Why? Because it hurts Him to see someone He loves feeling so miserable, and it pleases Him when we come to Him believing God Himself is the fullness we desire.

He will seize the opportunity our emptiness creates: just as Jesus healed the despairing father's daughter of a terminal illness, Papa will fill your empty heart. Discovered emptiness is our opportunity to learn what it means to know God, to relate to Him more deeply than we ever could with a terrific spouse, to enjoy Him more than chocolate pie or good friends, and to love Him with all our empty, hopeful, about-to-be-filled hearts.

How the PAPA Prayer Works

We can create that opportunity for God to fill our empty hearts by praying the PAPA prayer—by presenting, attending, and purging, and then with the emptiness we discover within our hearts, approaching God who longs to fill us with Himself. Here's how it works.

PRESENT YOURSELF TO GOD

Present yourself to God, honestly, over time, and two things will happen. You'll realize that you're not where you want to be, and you'll realize you're not who you want to be. You'll realize it with such force that you'll wake up to the terrifying fact that you can't get to where you want to be on your own and you can't make yourself who you want to be.

Where do you long to be? In a safe relationship, where you're so loved and so valued and so wanted that no rejection, disaster, or failure can destroy you. You want to find your identity in a community of perfect love where you belong.

Who do you yearn to be? An alive, whole person, someone who has the resources to be truly loving and truly good and truly strong in every circumstance, even with people who hurt you deeply.

The more honestly you face your red dot (where you are and who you are), the more you'll become aware of a holy space within you. I call it "holy" because it's a void filled with desire for what only God can provide. Counterfeit satisfaction can never fill it. Second-thing pleasures won't do.

When you're in touch with that holy space, you'll feel your longing for a guide who knows where you want to be and can take you there. And you'll be able to identify your yearning for a gentle healer, for someone who sees you as you are, who doesn't shrink away in disgust, who knows better than you who you most want to be, and has the power to transform you into that person.

Present yourself to God, and you'll discover your desire for a *guide* and a *healer*.

Attend to How You Are Thinking of God

Attend to how you are thinking of God, see how corrupted and self-serving your image of God is, and then look in the Bible for God as He really is (even when you're not immediately attracted to who you meet); and again two things will happen. From deep within you, in your holy space, you'll feel the emptiness of absolute terror and unrealized hope.

Who is this God? He can get really mad at people who disobey Him. You're not sure you want to be anywhere close to Him. He scares you. You'd just as soon ignore Him and get on with your life.

But no, you really don't want to do that. He's it. He's reality. He's everything. He's the boss. And He's good. You want to get close to Him. Is it possible? Would He destroy you? Do you dare hope that you could become intimate with this terrifying God who sometimes seems like a monster, and find out that He's the most wonderful Person in the universe?

Keep attending to who God is, and more desires in your holy space will become recognizable. You'll realize you long for a powerful king, big enough to intimidate you so completely that you end up fearing no one and nothing else but Him. And you'll know that you want a friend, a friend in high places whose companionship eliminates all fear, a friend who has the authority to welcome you into the throne room of the king as an invited guest, an adopted child, a royal heir.

Attend to how you're thinking of God, and you'll discover your desire for a *king* and a *friend*.

Purge Yourself of Anything That Blocks Your Relationship with God

Purge yourself of anything you see that blocks your relationship with God, examine the ways you sin relationally every day, and, as a broken person, you'll become aware of a deadly poison that is flowing freely in your holy space.

You'll discover energy within you, the energy of self-obsession, a snake pit of priority concern for your own well-being that trumps any concern for God's pleasure or the happiness of others. It's devious. It's subtle. It can look good. But when you see it in yourself, you'll actually learn to hate it more than you hate that same energy in your spouse or parent or friend.

You'll feel empty of goodness, thoroughly self-centered, committed to nothing greater than protecting yourself from feeling bad about yourself. But the space you've entered is holy. It was made by God, for God.

And out of that space, a desire will arise. It was there all the time, but now you can feel it. You're longing for a donor, someone with the pure energy of God-obsession, someone who knows the freedom to love that comes from first being loved by God and then loving Him, someone who loves you enough to give up His life in order to transplant that new energy in you.

You want to love. You want to be freed from the dungeon of self-obsession. And you realize you need a healthy donor, a truly good Person who can somehow pour His goodness into you, a goodness more powerful than the poison that's already there.

Purge yourself and you'll discover your desire for a *donor* of life.

Face your emptiness and you'll find your desire, human desire, holy desire. Present who you are to God, attend to how you see God and to who He really is, purge yourself of everything in you that gets in the way of your relationship with God, and you'll discover the holy space within you that only God can fill. You'll experience its emptiness.

And in that experience of emptiness, you'll get in touch with your desire for:

- a guide who can lead you into a world of perfect love;
- a healer who will transform you into that person you long to be;
- a king so powerful that you fear no one else, whose favor guarantees you everything you could ever want;

- a friend who draws you into depths of intimacy you never dreamed possible;
- a donor who is a perfect match, like you in every way except that His energy is God-obsessed, yours is self-obsessed; someone who is willing to make the ultimate sacrifice so you can live the way He lives, the way you long to live.

Well, I know you're way ahead of me. Everything we desire is available in relationship with Papa. Along with His Son and Spirit, He provides it all.

All that's left for us to do is approach God in our emptiness, desiring everything we were created to enjoy, confident that He will fill our emptiness and satisfy our desires—with Himself.

I illustrate what approaching God looks like in the next chapter, with a parable.

chapter nineteen

&

Become Someone God Can Really Enjoy

*F*or just a moment, fix your eyes on what you can't see. Tilt your ear toward the world of the Spirit, and listen in on a dialogue going on right now between you and God.

> God: I've kept a list of everything you've ever asked Me for. Some requests I've granted. Some I've denied. Look over the list, and add to it anything you would like to ask Me for now.
>
> You: Will You give me everything I ask for?
>
> God: Yes.
>
> You: But You didn't before. I've asked for lots of things You didn't give me.
>
> God: Every unanswered request was not a true prayer. Those petitions did not come from your heart.
>
> You: I don't understand.
>
> God: You will. Complete the list. Ask for anything you want.

Confused but excited, you read through the hundreds of prayers that contain every request you've ever made to God. You have asked for much, little things and big; things that mattered to you a great deal and things that you merely preferred, like good weather for your holiday picnic.

You're surprised at how many requests have been granted. You're grateful. But many requests, both big and little, have been denied. In some cases, you can now see a greater good was served because God didn't give you what you asked for.

But not in all. It still makes no sense why your son's heart was hardened when he was first caught smoking marijuana. And it's only gotten worse. You've prayed daily that he'll find God and return to the family.

That request is already on the list. It fills a dozen pages. But didn't God just say He would grant whatever request you add to the list? The story of the persistent petitioner comes to mind. You grab your pen, turn to the blank pages at the end of the sheaf of papers in front of you, and eagerly write:

> I want my son to become a Christian, to give up drugs, finish college, marry a wonderful Christian girl, develop into a godly husband and father, succeed in a worthwhile career, and live to advance God's kingdom. Amen!

Your heart races. God told you to ask away, for anything. You scribble more requests:

> Good health, no Alzheimer's, 20 percent annual growth in my pension fund, intimate marriage, lifelong friendships, renewed energy, no headaches.

Your imagination kicks into high gear. With the freedom of no embarrassment, your desires swing wildly between "good life" hopes and "spiritual" yearnings: a bigger house, a pure thought life, lots of money, deeper peace, exciting sex, powerful impact on others. Then God speaks again.

> God: Look deep into your heart. See if there are more desires you
> have not yet expressed.

You feel silly, but you write down your desire to eat what you want and
never gain weight, to exercise as little as you want and still get in good
shape, to convince your spouse he needs to be more sensitive, less critical,
and more appreciative of all you do.

As you read what you've just written, you become aware of deeper
desires stirring within you:

> I want a life full of meaning.
> I want my church to become a real community.
> I want to love my family better.
> I want to be a good grandparent.
> I want to be content, not greedy.
> I want to feel joy and hope and love.

Your dialogue with God continues:

> You: I'm finished, God. I can't think of anything more to add.
> God: You haven't yet discovered your heart.
> You: What do You mean?
> God: I told you I would give you whatever you want. Is this what
> you want?
> You: My list is complete. I have written down everything I want.
> God: Then I will give you everything on your list. But on one con-
> dition: you will never hear My voice again. I will withdraw all
> sense of My presence from you. You will never know Me.

Immediately, you tear up your list into little pieces. Thousands of requests
on hundreds of papers lie scattered on the ground in scraps all around you.

You fall down in the middle of them all.

> You: God, these are second things, all of them. I see it now. Yes,
> I want them. But they mean nothing if I don't have You.
>
> God: You have discovered your heart. You will now meet Me as
> your guide into love, your healer of selfishness, your king
> with all power, your friend in the highest place, your donor
> of life.

❖ ❖ ❖

Look at a simple picture. It expresses the point of the parable you've just read.

WHAT I WANT:	WHAT I WANT, BUT WANT LESS:
My List of FIRST THINGS	My List of SECOND THINGS
❖————————————❖	❖————————————❖
• Guide	• Everything else
• Healer	
• King	
• Friend	
• Donor	

= PAPA

The central point of prayer is to come to God for first things. As you learn to relationally pray, you will be more able to ask for second things and to mean it when you complete your request with the words, "If it's Your will." And your second-thing requests will grow out of your deepest desire to know God better.

THE FOUR-MINUTE PLAN FOR THE PAPA PRAYER

On pages 171–189, I outline what I call the Four-Day Plan, which you will find helpful in learning to pray the PAPA prayer. Follow the plan by yourself or, better yet, with your spouse, a friend, your small group, perhaps with a PAPA prayer group you form to learn how to relationally pray.

Let me suggest an even simpler way to get started. I call it the Four-Minute Plan.

When you wake up, spend one minute presenting to God whatever you're feeling or thinking about as your day begins. Ask for nothing. Just tell God what's happening inside you.

Spend the next minute attending to God. Who do you imagine you're talking to? A divine vending machine? An indifferent ruler? Think of one thing you know is true about God because the Bible says so. He's holy. Merciful. Just. Faithful. Love.

Then take a minute to ask yourself, "How am I not like God? How do I tend to relate: poorly, self-protectively, defensively, aggressively? How did I relate poorly yesterday?" Purge yourself by admitting it and calling it wrong.

In the fourth minute, come to God. Approach Him in your red dot that helps you be aware of how much more you want. Approach Him with an awareness of who He is that makes you both tremble and draw close. Approach Him knowing you've got a long way to go in becoming a really good person. Approach Him in your emptiness and desire. And that could mean saying something as simple as, "I really want You. I want lots of other things, but I want You most."

The four-minute plan is only a beginning. But it's a good beginning. Do it every day. The Four-Day Plan will take you further. You'll move from kindergarten and join me in first grade in the school of relational prayer. We'll move together into higher grades.

Approach God As Your First Thing

Now here's the promise. It's from God. When you come to God as your first thing, the full power of heaven will be released to bring you into a deeper relationship with God. That's what Jesus, Papa's Son, promised. Listen to His words: "If you believe, you will receive whatever you ask for in prayer" (Matthew 21:22).

Is He telling us that He'll see to it we receive everything on our second-thing wish list? I don't think so. Look at the context. He made that promise right after He cursed the fig tree. Matthew tells the story:

> Early in the morning, as he was on his way back to the city, he was hungry. Seeing a fig tree by the road, he went up to it but found nothing on it except leaves. Then he said to it, "May you never bear fruit again!" Immediately the tree withered.
>
> When the disciples saw this, they were amazed. "How did the fig tree wither so quickly?" they asked.
>
> Jesus replied, "I tell you the truth, if you have faith and do not doubt, not only can you do what was done to the fig tree, but also you can say to this mountain, 'Go, throw yourself into the sea,' and it will be done. If you believe, you will receive whatever you ask for in prayer." (Matthew 21:18–22)

Look closely at what happened. Jesus was hungry. It was morning, He and His friends were heading out on a long walk, and Jesus wanted breakfast. He spotted a fig tree and saw that it was "in leaf" early. It was spring, and fig trees didn't usually sprout leaves until June. Early leaves might mean early fruit. So Jesus went over to look.

When He pushed back the leaves and found no figs, He exploded, "You'll never bear fruit again!" Why? Was it petulant rage, what a spoiled child might do if her mother said, "No more cookies"? Of course not.

When He saw leaves, the evidence of life, but found no fruit, no life to enjoy, I think He felt His Father's pain.

In Hosea, God was reminiscing about His children when they were little. "When I found Israel, it was like finding grapes in the desert; when I saw your fathers, it was like seeing the *early fruit on the fig tree*" (Hosea 9:10; emphasis mine).

Listen to what I believe was going on inside Jesus: "My Father made people for Himself. He feels great pleasure when His children come to Him to find the fullness they desire. But people have become like the fig tree: lots of leaves but no fruit. Lots of religious activity, lots of people crowding into big buildings to hear the hot celebrity preacher, lots of concern for doing church right that's causing division, but only a few people who want nothing more than to come to Him.

"I will not have it! I will remove every mountain in their hearts that stands between them and My Father. I will put My life in their hearts so they can please Him as I please Him. There will be no more appearance of life without the reality of life, no more leaves without fruit."

And then He speaks, to us: "Friends, if you want to get close to My Father, I'll get you there. Ask Me for anything that will result in your becoming a ripe fig for My Father to enjoy, and I'll make sure you get it. It's what He most wants and it's what you'll realize you most want, when you discover your heart."

There is no greater joy for us than to become people our Papa can enjoy. Let's learn to pray the PAPA prayer, to relate to God as our first thing and to trust Him with however He decides to handle the second-thing requests.

chapter twenty

The PAPA Prayer: It's a Way of Life

*W*hen we mature enough to want from God what He's ready to give us, incredible things happen—sometimes around us, always in us. He *may* use His power to change our circumstances to our liking. He *will* use His power to change our hearts to His liking.

Down deep, that's what we want Him to do. He's taught us that getting close to Him is better than any blessing this world can provide. But there are a few mountains in our hearts blocking the road. We can't get around them to get to Him. They need to be moved, thrown into the sea.

That's what He's promised to do: to clear the road. He'll remove all those mountains of self-obsession, those peaks of too-strong affections for second things, those jagged cliffs of bitterness over the way we've been treated. He'll throw them all into the sea. If we ask Him—if that's what we want, that's what He'll do.

And then, when we walk the cleared path into His presence, He'll see to it that we get there and bear fruit. No more leaves with no figs for Papa to enjoy. That's the guarantee. If we ask Him—if that's what we want, that's what He'll do.

What Happens When You Pray the PAPA Prayer?

Let's review what's been happening in you—or will happen—as you learn to pray relationally, as you approach Papa to receive what He's ready to give.

You're becoming more honest about what's going on in you, in your thoughts and intentions and emotional reactions.

You're complaining less to people because you're sharing more with God. Pouring your heart out to God keeps you from dumping as much on your family and friends.

You're dropping the religious phoniness, the pseudospiritual posturing, the pretense that everything is just great. You're confessing your secret sins with less resistance, with more desire to stop them; and you're talking about them with Papa when you're ready to commit them again.

You're admitting who's driving you crazy, how ticked you are at your spouse and your frustrating kid. You're putting into words how lonely and disillusioned you sometimes feel at church, how you occasionally slide down into a dark hole where you can see no light.

This is the Christian life? The spiritual journey? You're not always sure. But you find yourself more in touch with how you're grateful for small things like an hour by yourself at a coffee shop, and for big things like the promise of heaven, of an end to all the weariness and struggle. And you're telling God that too.

You've been *presenting* your red dot to Papa.

You're becoming a little more (maybe a lot more) awed by who God is. You're seeing Him more clearly in Jesus, the Jesus with fiery eyes that burn right through you, that bore through every wall of self-protection you've built; the Jesus with a scalpel-shaped sword hanging out of His mouth like a sharp tongue waiting to cut away whatever

He finds offensive, ready to wither all those spiritual leaves that wrongly convince everyone there must be fruit in your life.

You're realizing how often you think of God as a doting grandfather you can play to your advantage, or as a high and mighty monarch who pays no attention to how your life is going. And that realization, that you're thinking of God so wrongly, has left you a bit uncomfortable, embarrassed.

But you're more awed by God than ashamed of yourself. You're beginning to recognize God as a bewildering yet strangely beckoning blend of intimidating might and compassionate warmth, of terrifying holiness and welcoming grace, of seemingly erratic sensitivity and actually unfailing love.

You're not sure whether to fall at His feet or dance. But you're certainly not bored or casual in your prayers, or frivolous in your worship.

You're *attending* to who Papa really is.

You're being more painfully humbled by a fresh awareness of how self-obsessed you really are.

What you thought was legitimate distress now carries into your nostrils the odor of self-centeredness. You're more conscious of the subtle ways in which you fall short of God-obsessed living. When your spouse asks you to do something that is inconvenient, you now recognize the stench of your self-obsession rather than wonder why he or she is so demanding.

Some of your wrestling matches with God over those things in your life that are ripping apart your soul, those heated exchanges about what He's not doing, are now being revealed to you as demands for your sake, not desire for His glory. Self-obsession leaks out of even your holiest moments. You just didn't see it before. Now you do.

But it's not depressing you; it's releasing you. Now that you see brokenness as more than woundedness and struggle, now that you're broken over how far you have to go to become like Jesus, holy desires long buried are rising to the surface.

From deeper places than you knew existed, the desire to love more sacrificially is bubbling up. More than anything else, your new experience of brokenness is releasing a passionate desire to be closer to God. You're abandoning yourself to holiness. You're discovering that you want what God most wants to give.

You're entering a new level of the *purging* process.

And now you're talking to God, believing something wonderful is on the way; something is coming that you'll enjoy receiving as much as He'll enjoy giving.

You're coming to Him not to get Him to enter your world and change things to make you happy and give your life meaning and provide you with the blessings you want. You're now entering His world wanting to bring Him glory, to become a source of joy to your Papa, willing to endure whatever suffering is required to make that happen.

And it's having surprising results. The more you long to bring Him joy, the more you're experiencing joy yourself. But it's a new kind of joy, a settled quietness that has nothing to prove, a solid sense of your self that you know is real only because of your relationship with Papa, a different kind of joy that makes all other happiness seem shallow. It's not there all the time, but its possibility is always there. And you sense it's always around the corner. So you hang on.

And you hang on with certainty, with genuineness, with faith that anchors hope. You're finding your center, the reality, the privilege, the hope of knowing God better. In the process, you're discovering who you truly are. You're realizing that you're a significant, secure, vital, real person who cannot be destroyed, someone who is on your way to becoming a really good person.

You care more about others than you used to. Your grudges are thinner, your worries less consuming. You're daring to hope that you're on course toward your destiny, to becoming God-obsessed, to love Him above every other good, and to love others for His sake and theirs, not yours. Just like Jesus.

You're *approaching* God.

There. That's the PAPA prayer so far. But there's more.

LEARNING TO PUT FIRST THINGS FIRST

You've been praying the PAPA prayer, and your heart thumps as you read these words from Hebrews: "So, friends, we can now—without hesitation—walk right up to God. . . . Jesus has cleared the way. . . . So let's do it—full of belief, confident that we're presentable inside and out" (Hebrews 10:19–22 MSG).

You read on, and your heart thumps louder. "Now that we know what we have—Jesus, this great High Priest with ready access to God—let's not let it slip through our fingers. [The writer is talking about our opportunity to know God and to get what He wants to give.] We don't have a priest who is out of touch with our reality. . . . [Jesus saw you crying last night; He's already told Papa about it.] So let's walk right up to him and get what he is so ready to give" (Hebrews 4:14–16 MSG).

So what is it? What's Papa giving? And is it what we really want?

We will receive everything we need to live the way we long to live, the way we were destined to live. We will receive everything we need to become who we truly are, not abuse victims or sex addicts or desperate housewives or incurable failures, but Papa's children.

We will receive everything we need to hear His voice, to hear our happy Papa turn to the angels of heaven and the demons of hell and say,

"See him? He wants Me more than anything else. See her? Look how she responds to people who treat her badly. Isn't that beautiful? She's doing it for Me. Take a look. I'm raising wonderful children."

And we'll receive the spiritual ears we need to listen as He turns to each of us, individually, and says, "You are My son. You are My daughter. I'm well pleased. I not only love you, but I like you. I enjoy your company."

When your precious little girl lies sick in a hospital bed, what do you want the most? To see God's power heal her? Or to hear God's voice provide you with everything you need to honor Him whether she lives or dies?

If you want her healing more than you want to know God and live for His pleasure, you'll miss out on what God is ready to give. Your daughter might be healed. Of course you want that. Of course you should pray for it. That prayer, however, might not be answered. But the power to glorify God whatever happens will be given—if you approach God, ready to receive what He's ready to give. That's a promise.

Praying the PAPA prayer rearranges our values. It helps us put first things first, and to keep second things out of first place and in second place where they belong.

A Personal Example of the PAPA Prayer

Let me end on a personal note, with one more story of how I'm learning to pray the PAPA prayer.

It's now six thirty in the morning. I'm sitting in my bathrobe in front of the fireplace, writing these words. Earlier this morning, from three till about four thirty, I wrestled with God. I don't think I've ever before experienced prayer as I just did.

I felt terrible yesterday, from midafternoon on. My head hurt. Fatigue was so extreme that eating dinner was a chore. And I felt empty, isolated, weightless. I wasn't sure what I believed about myself, life, or God. I have no idea what triggered it all. Looking back, from the perspective of morning, I believe it was a spiritual battle.

When I awoke at three, I felt desperate. Miserable. I had to know God better. I thought of God's words through Hosea: "In their misery they will earnestly seek me" (5:15).

I begged God to meet me, to let me meet Him. I thought about all that was happening in me and in my life, and I told all of it to God. I pictured Jesus the way He revealed Himself to John in Revelation. Then I made my way mentally through the books of the Bible, trying to remember how God revealed Himself and what He did in each one. I saw Him high and lifted up when I got to Isaiah, and I felt small, weak, corrupted.

I kept saying over and over, "I'm here. I don't know what else to do. If You don't meet me, I can't make it. You're all I have. I believe You're all I need."

When I reached Hebrews, this verse appeared in my mind like a flashing billboard: "Anyone who comes to him [God] must believe that he exists and that he rewards those who earnestly seek him" (11:6). In that verse I heard my Papa's voice.

"God, I believe. Help my unbelief. Papa, I'm drawing near to You as best I know how. Please draw near to me."

At about four thirty, I stopped praying. I lay in bed till five, too exhausted to get up, but no longer desperate. Like someone in a dark room standing behind you whom you can't see but whose presence you feel, Papa was there. I knew it. Jesus's words flooded into my mind: "Be of good cheer. I have overcome the world" (John 16:33 KJV). Again, that was my Papa's voice.

I felt safe, in good hands. I remember saying to myself, "I no longer feel desperate. I'm at peace. I feel hope. And joy."

But I didn't move. I wanted more sleep. Then, at five, I heard a clanging noise, the sound two garbage can lids would make if they were smashed together like cymbals. The noise was muted, but it seemed to come from inside our home.

I wondered what it was, a little worried that water pipes were bursting or something had fallen. But I didn't move. I wanted more sleep. I heard the noise again. When the sound came a third time, I got up.

The sound stopped. I didn't hear it again. I knew its source. The Spirit was telling me to get my tired body out of bed and write this chapter. I know that sounds weird, strange, fantastic. But if God wants to make noise like garbage can lids banging together, I guess He can. I had been trying to write for six days. Nothing came. Just forty or fifty pages of paper filled with scribbles that meant nothing, made no sense.

"I'm flowing through you. I'm giving you the chapter. Get up and write." Again, Papa was speaking to me through His Spirit.

I was still tired. I still wanted more sleep. But I wanted to get up. I didn't bother to shower or brush my teeth. I couldn't wait to get my pad of paper and pen.

Dressed in my bathrobe that has the word *Pop* sewn onto it (a gift from my three grandkids), I came downstairs, poured a little wine into a glass, broke a piece of bread from a loaf, and knelt before the fireplace.

I read from 1 Corinthians 11: "What you must solemnly realize is that every time you eat this bread and every time you drink this cup, you re-enact in your words and actions the death of the Master" (v. 26 MSG).

I read on. "If you give no thought (or worse, don't care) about the broken body of the Master when you eat and drink, you're running the risk of serious consequences" (v. 29 MSG).

As I knelt, with the bread and wine on the hearth in front of me, I trembled. Do I care that Jesus died? Do I care more that my daughter-in-law's pregnancy goes well, that the weather cooperates with my golf plans this afternoon, that my neck pain goes away, that everyone in our family stays healthy?

Like a gentle thunderbolt, the thought struck me: I couldn't have approached God as my Papa for the last several hours if Jesus hadn't died. I'd be stuck looking for relief from my emotional pain some other way, scrambling to feel better for reasons that couldn't amount to much.

But because Jesus died and rose my judge is now my Papa. I have a guide and a healer. God is now my king and my friend. And I have God's life in me. He's my donor as well. I'm in the royal family. And, as I receive the sacrament, I can confidently ask Him to stir the life that's in me and pour it out of me, through my words as I write for the next couple of hours. That was Papa's voice.

I ate the bread and drank the wine. I didn't tremble. I didn't cry. I smiled. I could hear my heart respond with an overwhelming *yes!* It's all true! The bottom line is good. I can walk right up to God, the same God who divided the Red Sea and raised Jesus from the dead, and get what He wants to give me.

And I can pick up my pen and tell you all about it. That's when I decided to end this chapter on a personal note, to tell you how God used the PAPA prayer to carry me from despair to joy.

The joy is real. The despair is gone, though not completely. Joy that comes from the Spirit never eliminates pain; it takes its place at the center. Until heaven. Then it fills everything, every place, every relationship.

For now, I still groan. Life is not what I want it to be. I'm not who I want to be. But right now I know—I *know*—that I'm loved. I'm accepted; God is not discarding me, He's preparing me; I'm wanted and I matter; I have the weightiness of one who is called to be part of the most important thing going on in the world today.

Nothing can change that. But we don't always see it. We don't always know it. Sometimes we don't see it at all. Sometimes we wonder if it's really true.

That's where I was yesterday afternoon and evening. That's where I was when I woke up at three this morning. That's where I'll be again, and again and again till I get home.

But now, this moment, it's not where I am. I'm filled with joy. And hope. And peace. I know it's possible to feel this way, in the middle of difficult emotions. It's the fruit of the Spirit.

And it's what your Papa wants to give you, no matter what is happening in your life. And He will give it to you. Come to Him to receive what He's eager to give. Come empty. Come with your desires. Come believing. Learn to pray the PAPA prayer. You'll discover the sound of your Father's voice.

Practical Helps
FOR LEARNING TO PRAY
THE PAPA PRAYER

A Simple Four-Day Plan

*O*nce you get a feel for it, praying relationally comes as naturally as breathing. Relating to God is what we were designed to do.

But the feel doesn't come so easily. We've grown accustomed to thinking of prayer as our chance to get from God whatever we believe we need (or want) to live satisfying and meaningful lives. Learning to pray as our primary means of relating to God requires intentionality. It takes some practice.

So I've developed a plan to get you started. The plan is really a synthesis of what I've been clumsily doing for nearly a year to make relational prayer the center of my life. It's a simple plan, one that requires only a little time during four days.

Of course, it's only a beginning, but the journey from the city to the beach begins with the first few steps. I'm suggesting four steps in what I call the Four-Day Plan.

Day 1: Learning to *present* yourself to God
Day 2: Learning to *attend* to how you are thinking of God
Day 3: Learning to *purge* yourself of anything that blocks your relationship with God

Day 4:   Learning to *approach* God as the "first thing" in your life

For each day, the plan provides four things:

1. A learning objective, contrasted with what you may need to unlearn.
2. A Bible passage to read and ponder first thing in the morning, along with a brief discussion of the key point of the passage as it relates to the part of the PAPA prayer being considered that day.
3. A reflection question about the passage to ask yourself throughout the day in order to direct your attention to the prayer focus for that day.
4. An illustration of that day's prayer focus designed to guide you in writing your own prayer before you go to bed.

Begin any day you choose. If you're going to follow the plan with your spouse, friend, or small group (which I strongly suggest), then you should all begin the Four-Day Plan on the same day so you can better track your experiences with each other. It's essential that everyone read and discuss *The PAPA Prayer* before beginning the Four-Day Plan.

Is all that clear? You'll be learning to identify and verbalize your red dot on day 1.

On day 2, you'll take a look at who you envision God to be when you pray, and you'll compare that picture to who the Bible reveals God to be.

Day 3 might be painful, but it will be liberating. You'll be asking God's Spirit to reveal to you who or what you value more than God.

And finally, on day 4, you'll claim your privilege as God's son or daughter by walking right up to Him in order to enjoy relating to Him. You'll find a few mountains blocking your path, but ask Jesus to hurl them into the sea. He will.

DAY 1:
LEARNING TO PRESENT YOURSELF TO GOD

Learning Objective
Present authentically to God whatever you discover in yourself, whether good or bad.

Don't hold anything back.

Don't pretend that what's going on inside you (e.g. hatred) really isn't happening.

Don't trivialize what's happening as unimportant, petty, not worth mentioning.

Don't spin whatever you discover that's disagreeable into something more pleasant.

Stand in your red dot.
Be who you are, where you are.

Bible Passage (Read first thing on day 1.)

No doubt about it! God is good—good to good people, good to the good-hearted.

But I nearly missed it, missed seeing his goodness.

I was looking the other way, looking up to the people at the top, envying the wicked who have it made,

Who have nothing to worry about, not a care in the whole wide world.

Pretentious with arrogance, they wear the latest fashions in violence.

Pampered and overfed, decked out in silk bows of silliness.

They jeer, using words to kill; they bully their way with words.

They're full of hot air, loudmouths disturbing the peace.

People actually listen to them—can you believe it? Like thirsty puppies, they lap up their words.

What's going on here? Is God out to lunch? Nobody's tending the store.

The wicked get by with everything; they have it made, piling up riches.

I've been stupid to play by the rules; what has it gotten me?

A long run of bad luck, that's what—a slap in the face every time I walk out the door.

If I'd given in and talked like this, I would have betrayed your dear children.

Still, when I tried to figure it out, all I got was a splitting headache.
(Psalm 73:1–16 MSG; if you have time, read it also in other translations.)

Key Point: Living according to God's principles doesn't guarantee the blessings you want. Living for yourself in this world seems to work better.

The psalmist knew he could discourage younger Christians if he told them what he was thinking. But he told God, and the Spirit saw to it that he left a record of what he told God to encourage us to present ourselves authentically to God. He knew where presenting oneself to God led—to the sanctuary, where the psalmist discovered that what he really wanted was God. Read the rest of the psalm.

Reflection Question (Ponder throughout day 1.)

What am I thinking and feeling right now . . .

• as I'm talking with this person?

• as I'm walking through this store?

• as I'm watching television?

• as I'm praying or reading my Bible?

Illustration of Presenting Yourself to God (Reflect and journal on the evening of day 1.)

Mark's life is going well: a wife he loves, three great kids, wonderful sales job that pays well, a respected role in his church as an elder and talented vocalist.

The doctor discovers nodules in Mark's throat that may be malignant. Mark tells his wife that God can be trusted. He feels safe in God's care.

The night before the biopsy, he wakes up with a panic attack. He tries to calm himself by saying that God knows his sales job and his musical gift both require a strong voice. Suddenly he realizes he has no guarantee that the nodules will be benign.

He presents himself to God: "It makes no sense to me that You might let me have throat cancer. I have no guarantee I'll ever speak or sing again. That terrifies me. And it seems so unfair. I've served You well all my life. I'm really angry, and scared. I have no idea in the world how to trust You. All this talk of knowing You better in hard times seems empty to me right now—and irritating."

Your experience might reflect the same spirit of entitlement to second things that surfaced in Mark. Or you might be aware of real peace in hard times or humble gratitude in good times.

Hold nothing back.
Pretend about nothing.
Don't trivialize anything.
Spin nothing that's ugly into something pretty.
Be completely honest with God.

Stand in your red dot.
Be who you are, where you are.

Present yourself to God in writing. Write out your own prayer.

DAY 2:
LEARNING TO ATTEND TO HOW YOU ARE THINKING OF GOD

Learning Objective

Attend to who God really is (as revealed in the Bible) versus who you think God is (based on life experience) or who you want Him to be (based on your felt desires).

Don't assume your view of God is correct.

Don't project your experience with authority figures, especially your father, onto God.

Don't sugarcoat the word *God* to satisfy your desire for a pleasant experience with Him.

Don't believe everything you hear, except from God Himself in the Bible.

Stand before the God of the Bible.
You'll fall to your knees, but you'll get up a new person.

Bible Passage (Read first thing on day 2.)

These are rebellious people, deceitful children, children unwilling to listen to the LORD's instruction. They say to the seers, "See no more visions!" and to the prophets, "Give us no more visions of what is right! Tell us pleasant things, prophesy illusions. Leave this way, get off this path, and stop confronting us with the Holy One of Israel!" (Isaiah 30:9–11)

In the year that King Uzziah died, I saw the LORD seated on a throne, high and exalted, and the train of his robe filled the temple. Above him were seraphs, each with six wings: With two wings they covered

their faces, with two they covered their feet, and with two they were
flying. And they were calling to one another:

"Holy, holy, holy is the LORD Almighty; the whole earth is full
of his glory."

At the sound of their voices the doorposts and thresholds shook and
the temple was filled with smoke. (Isaiah 6:1–4)

Key Point: Our consuming desire for second things makes us want to
see God as nothing more than their friendly provider. Until we see God as
unapproachably holy, we will not concern ourselves with the first thing of
how we, sinful people, can relate to the holy God.

Isaiah had a difficult life. He delivered a message that his culture did
not want to hear. The strength to remain faithful in his preaching and in
his life came from seeing God as He really is, a holy God that required
Isaiah to deal with one issue before all others: how can a self-obsessed man
become God-obsessed? Isaiah 6:5–8 gives the answer. Forgiveness provided by God releases a person to surrender everything to God. It all
started with a clear picture of who God is.

Reflection Question (Ponder throughout day 2.)

How am I picturing God right now . . .

- as I'm asking Him to bless me?
- as I'm facing this trial?
- as I'm sitting in church?
- as I'm arguing with a friend?

Illustration of Attending to Your Picture of God (Reflect and journal on
the evening of day 2.)

Brenda has struggled for a long time with her relationship to God.
Her dad left the family when she was thirteen, after her mother caught

him sexually abusing Brenda. Brenda's first husband regularly watched pornography on the Internet and never approached her for sex.

When they divorced, she began going to church and trusted Christ. She met a wonderful man, married, had three kids, earned a counseling degree, and developed a ministry to abused and divorced women. She still struggled with depression and nightmares but was deeply grateful for the work God had done in her life.

Her husband (then a deacon) confessed to adultery and was truly repentant. Four months after his confession, their seventeen-year-old daughter announced she was pregnant. The church had already asked her husband to resign as deacon. She was now asked to step down from her ministry role to women, which had become a paid staff position in her church.

She attends to how she visualizes God: "God, I've trusted You all these years. I still trust You. But I'm so surprised that all this has happened. Somehow being let go by the church, and not feeling wanted there, is more painful than even my husband's affair or our daughter's pregnancy.

"I guess I've thought of You as some blend of a doting grandfather and a vending machine. Otherwise I wouldn't be so surprised at all that's happened. I want to see You now as You really are, the Holy God who owes me nothing but gives me heaven, my Papa whom I can trust to keep me trusting, my Papa who loves me, who loves me like You love Your Son.

"Coming to Your Son with that sword in His mouth doesn't sound like much fun, but that's what I want to do. I want to know Your light is shining in my heart, no matter how much it hurts."

Your picture of God is distorted. Assume that. Everyone's is. But you want to know God as He really is. Assume that too. His Spirit is in you,

longing to reveal your Papa to you. The Spirit knows how wonderful
He is.

Don't assume your view of God is correct.

Realize your experience with authority figures has shaped your view of
God.

Identify your tendency to create God into someone who will always
help you feel good.

Always check out your impressions of God—and what you've been
told—with Scripture.

Stand before the God of the Bible.
You'll fall to your knees, but you'll get up a new person.

Attend to God in writing. Write out your own prayer.

_____
_____
_____
_____
_____
_____
_____
_____
_____
_____
_____
_____
_____

DAY 3:
LEARNING TO PURGE YOURSELF OF ANYTHING THAT BLOCKS
YOUR RELATIONSHIP WITH GOD

Learning Objective
Purge whatever is blocking your intimacy with God by acknowledging without excuse or explanation the self-obsession staining your motives that the Spirit chooses to reveal.

Don't simply try hard to be good; don't merely promise to do better.

Don't criticize others' faults without first seeing your own equally serious faults.

Don't redefine your self-obsession into understandable mistakes.

Don't assume that your strong passion for what you believe is right is necessarily holy.

Stand naked before holiness.
The more you see your sin, the more you'll be amazed by grace.

Bible Passage (Read first thing on day 3.)

Investigate my life, O God, find out everything about me;
Cross-examine and test me, get a clear picture of what I'm about;
See for yourself whether I've done anything wrong—then guide me
on the road to eternal life. (Psalm 139:23–24 MSG)

Key Point: Nobody moves toward real Christlikeness without humility. Humility is not a bad self-image or a nonassertive personality. Humility is an eager willingness to see where you are wrong in order to experience the power of God that has already made you fit for His presence.

David, the psalmist, was an imperfect man. Like all of us, he preferred to not face his faults. When he committed adultery and murder, he tried to hide it. But when a godly friend confronted him, he owned his sin. Even more, he recognized that his sinful deeds came out of sinful roots in his heart. Behavioral change wasn't all that was required. A broken heart leading to repentance was necessary. (Read Psalm 51.)

Reflection Question (Ask throughout day 3.)

How am I obsessed with myself (my needs, my feelings, my convenience) right now . . .

- as I'm struggling with discouragement?
- as I'm handling this tension with my spouse or friend?
- as I'm anxious over what might happen?
- as I'm feeling disillusioned and bored with my church?

Illustration of Purging Yourself of Whatever Blocks the Relationship (Reflect and journal on the evening of day 3.)

Kyle is a Christian leader. He has been used by God to encourage and bless many people for many years. But Kyle is desperately insecure. He knows it and admits it to trusted friends, but he won't explore it. Because he's well respected and effective in ministry, he is able to convince himself that his insecurity is not a real problem.

His wife, Emily, leveled with him. After years of marriage, she admitted she doesn't feel safe with him and worries constantly that the next ministry conflict will tip him over the edge or drive him further into denial. She also told him their twenty-two-year-old son has said more than once that he sees his dad as a weak man, friendly and affirming, but unwilling to deal with tough stuff in their relationship. That got to him.

Kyle purges himself before God: "I've been afraid of rejection all my life. But I've found a way to win acceptance from people that has kept me from facing how determined I am to protect myself from rejection.

"God, I've always felt like a little boy nobody could want or respect. And enjoying the respect of influential people has become my first thing. Is that what's really going on? What am I not seeing here, God? I want to see every way I value anything more than I value You. And I want to see how my terrified stubbornness keeps me from touching the hearts of the people I love most."

In some way, your terror of being a weightless man who impacts no one deeply or an invisible woman whom no one sees and enjoys is affecting the way you relate. You're determined to experience the satisfaction of feeling valued and wanted more than you're determined to please God, to enjoy His worth, and to reach others with His life, no matter what they think of you.

Forget any self-improvement program.

Stop explaining why some people aren't drawn to you by reminding yourself how insecure and narrow-minded they are.

See the depraved self-centeredness beneath your personal and relational struggles; don't see yourself as a victim who needs to be understood.

Be open to the possibility that your strongest passions, even the "godly ones," have less to do with God's Spirit (who promotes God-obsession) than your flesh (the energy of self-obsession).

Stand naked before holiness.
The more you see your sin, the more you'll be amazed by grace.

Purge yourself before God in writing. Write out your own prayer.

Day 4:
Learning to Approach God As the
"First Thing" in Your Life

Learning Objective
Approach God with confidence that what He loves to give you is what you want the most.

Don't retreat from God when He seems unresponsive.

Don't negotiate with God. You have no leverage other than His relentless, tender love and your longing to get what He's giving.

Don't demand anything from God; expect the gift of relationship.

Don't let the desires that you feel dictate your expectations of what He'll give you.

Stand before God as a loved child.
Rest in His love as a prelude to receiving His best.

Bible Passage (Read first thing on day 4.)

I will heal their waywardness. I will love them lavishly. My anger is played out.

I will make a fresh start with Israel. He'll burst into bloom like a crocus in the spring.

He'll put down deep oak tree roots, he'll become a forest of oaks!

He'll become splendid—like a giant sequoia, his fragrance like a grove of cedars!

Those who live near him will be blessed by him, be blessed and prosper like golden grain.

Everyone will be talking about them, spreading their fame as the vintage children of God.

Ephraim is finished with gods that are no-gods. From now on I'm the one who answers and satisfies him.

I am like a luxuriant fruit tree. Everything you need is to be found in me.

If you want to live well, make sure you understand all of this.

If you know what's good for you, you'll learn this inside and out.

God's paths get you where you want to go. Right-living people walk them easily; wrong-living people are always tripping and stumbling. (Hosea 14:4–9 MSG)

Key Point: Everything you were designed to experience and enjoy is found in God. Knowing God is your life and your highest joy. You either believe that or you don't. Believe it and you will experience and enjoy life, real life, eventually. Guaranteed. Disbelieve it and, at best, you will experience counterfeit life and enjoy it only for a season.

These staggering promises from God are offered to people who repent. Read Hosea 14:1–3 for clear directions on what it means to repent. (Read Hosea 6:1–3 for an example of false repentance, where the people's focus is on their need for satisfaction, not their need for forgiveness.) Only when you present yourself authentically to God, attend to who He is, and purge yourself of self-obsession will you approach God to humbly and gratefully receive the greatest gift of all: a relationship with God as your Papa!

Reflection Question (Ponder throughout day 4.)

What does my heart most long for right now . . .

- as I enjoy time with my family and friends?
- as I wait for the lab report from my doctor?
- as I face criticism from colleagues?
- as I search for a better job?

Illustration of Approaching God As Your "First Thing" (Reflect and journal on the evening of day 4.)

Sarah is eighty-four years old. She is a widow, living in a home for senior adults who need assistance with everyday living. Her one daughter is divorced, childless, and lives far away, both from Sarah and from the Lord.

Sarah has never known such loneliness. She cries every night in her small room. She pours out her heart to God; she sees Him as the holy God who is with her and promises the best is yet to come; and she is disgusted with how petty and impatient she can be at dinner with the other residents.

She approaches God: "I know You're my Papa. I know You're with me. It's hard, Lord, harder than I ever imagined it would be. But I know Jesus is with You right now, and because I'm in Him, I'm with You too.

"And I know He's praying for me, and You're listening to every word. Some of His prayers are my cleaned-up words. So I come to You knowing You're aware of every tear I cry, every ache in my heart.

"I come. I come to You, Papa, hoping You'll take me home soon. But until You do, I come wanting every mountain that I can't climb to be lowered so I can feel Your arms around me. And when I can't feel them, I still come to You knowing You're supplying the faith I need to believe I'm in good hands, the hope I need to go on, and the love I need to let all these old folks know what You're like. Thank You, Papa. I know You're giving it all to me, everything, life! I love You."

Your circumstances are different from Sarah's. For a few of you, they're nearly identical. Many of you will one day know what Sarah is experiencing.

None of you is home. All of you live with desires that are not and cannot be satisfied. So stop living for satisfaction. Renounce your pursuit of comfort. Walk past the broken cisterns of this world and move toward the living water, toward God Himself.

Come to Him to get what He so loves to give—the first thing, the best thing—relationship with Himself. Enjoy all the second things in your life. Thank God for them. But never mistake them for life.

Approach God even when it seems He isn't there.

Stop offering God this if He'll do that. No bargaining with God.

Realize that if you demand fair treatment, you'll never see His face; if you live for second things, you'll not get to know God very well.

Trust no desire within you except your desire to know God.

Stand before God as a loved child.
Rest in His love as a prelude to receiving His best.

Approach God in writing. Write out your own prayer.

_____

_____

_____

_____

_____

_____

_____

_____

_____

_____

That's the Four-Day Plan. Repeat it as often as you like, as often as it's helpful. Revise it any way that is both consistent with its purpose and helpful to you. Relate to others your struggles to learn the PAPA prayer, as well as your happy experiences of moving into closer relationship with God.

Follow the plan. Learn to pray the PAPA prayer. And you will discover the sound of your Father's voice. You will discover the life of God in your soul.

A Special Word to Women

I know you don't like to think of yourself as a little girl. It's so demeaning. Chauvinistic. You're a grown woman, of equal worth to any man.

Of course you are. But deep in your feminine soul, you long to be held and delighted in by your real Papa. You're vulnerable, and you know it. Without strong love to rest in, you live defensively.

Until you present yourself to your real Papa as the little girl that you are, as the dependent, helpless, vulnerable child everyone is before God, you will never relate to anyone else as the whole, secure, talented, competent, beautiful woman God's love has made you.

Let the PAPA prayer become your opportunity to embrace, with neither shame nor fear, your absolute and total vulnerability. You know deep in your soul that without your Papa's love, you are an empty shell, an imposter who covers her fear with aggressive relating or manipulative shyness.

You live in terror. Exposure of who you really are would destroy you. No one would want you. You hate your weakness, your dependence, your neediness. It makes you so afraid. But what you really hate is your inescapable status as a dependent daughter of God.

That's why you cover yourself with religion and never stand naked before God. But until you do, you'll never discover that you've already been clothed with His strength, His beauty, His indestructibility.

Little girls think that they can overcome their dependent natures by growing up, by leaving dependency behind and becoming independent in their own resources. So they live to protect themselves, to prove themselves, to keep the promise they made to themselves as little girls to never hurt again like they once did.

But that strategy blocks you from loving anyone but yourself. Until you come as the dependent child you are to God, not to others, to the only One whose love can release you into maturity, you'll never be the unthreatened, undemanding, unselfish woman you were created to be.

So come. Come to God as a little girl so you can come to others as a whole woman.

Don't come to others as a little girl. That demeans you and manipulates them. And don't come to others as a woman entitled to better treatment, a woman who should be recognized for her abilities and loved for her value. Come first to God as the person you really are—scared, alone, and desperately dependent.

Embrace your worst fear, your deepest hurt, your terrifying dependence. Talk about it with God, honestly, without restraint, every day, whenever you become aware of it. That's presenting prayer, and it requires that you talk a lot. Don't just listen for God to speak. Begin the conversation by telling Him who you are.

Then picture who it is you're talking to. It's God, the same God who revealed Himself in Jesus when the glorified Christ reached down and touched His trembling servant John on Patmos and said, "Don't be afraid. Stand up."

That's His word to you. And you'll hear it during attending prayer. Stand up. You are a whole woman. But you will experience yourself as nothing more than a little girl until you feel His touch. And when you do, you can live with unassailable dignity, with feminine power that reveals a side of God no man can as fully reveal.

As you hear your Father's voice call you to womanhood, you'll become aware of how you hide your dependence behind aggressiveness and control, or shyness and retreat. You'll see how you've been protecting yourself, effectively telling God He's not enough, that you'll take over responsibility for your own well-being.

Call it what it is. It's sin. You're living to reduce your fear, to numb your pain, to feel accepted. It's all about you. Confess it to your Papa. He's already forgiven you. He's already smiling. He's already singing. You'll see His smile and hear His song when you engage in purging prayer.

Then you'll want to come to Him in approaching prayer, to run to Him like the prodigal, to depend on Him to become the woman you long to be. "God, I've been hiding my utter dependence behind my efforts to control. I've been committed to never feeling like a helpless little girl.

"But that's who I am. Admitting it and coming to You is my salvation. So I do come, as your vulnerable daughter, scared, weak, sinful. I come to You. I depend on You to forgive me for being so self-obsessed, for trying to handle my life with my own resources; and I trust You to release me from my prison of fear and helplessness into the liberty of the daughters of God."

Let the PAPA prayer become your lifestyle, your daily conversation with God. Come as a little girl to your Papa, so you can come to others as a real woman, a woman of unblemished beauty and unconquerable courage.

A Special Word to Men

$\mathcal{I}$ know it's hard to admit, and it's sometimes hard to get in touch with, but deep inside, hidden behind polo shirts, BMWs, paraded competence, social demeanor, intellectual conversations, and a lot of God-talk, you feel like a little boy.

A physician told me, "When I take off my white doctor's jacket and drive home from the hospital, I become a different person. When I walk in the front door, I feel like an embryo in the womb. I don't want to do anything or take care of anybody. I want someone to look after me. That's so pathetic. Is that why I stay up late to look at pornography on my computer?"

A businessman said, "I'm often in the head chair at the conference table where million-dollar deals are made. I'm known as hard-hitting, always prepared, relationally skilled—I get things done. No one knows I sometimes run to the bathroom to gear myself up. I feel like an imposter, a little boy in a man's suit. What I really want is for someone to like me, to approve of me. I hate that feeling. It's so weak."

Be honest. Deep in your heart, you sometimes feel scared, alone. Just like you felt when you were in grade school. Until you present yourself to your real Papa as the little boy that you still feel yourself to be, you'll never relate to anyone as the whole, unthreatened, unique, influential man that God's acceptance has already made you.

Let the PAPA prayer become your opportunity to embrace, with neither shame nor fear, the little boy in you that for so long has been hidden. Experiencing the pleasure and respect of your Papa is your only hope of true manhood. Without it, you're nothing but a mannequin in a store window—well built, well dressed, and lifeless.

But you're afraid. Me too. If you admit how scared you really are, no one will be there for you. You'll be seen as weak, pitiful, pathetic. And people will back away or come to you with demeaning sympathy that only makes matters worse.

But God responds differently. So come to Him. Don't parade your insecurities to everyone you meet. But don't hide them either.

That's likely what you've been doing. You hate your neediness, so you cover it up beneath macho conversations about who's going to win the Super Bowl or religious conversations about why you're reformed in your theology or political conversations about why Rush Limbaugh is an idiot or one of the few clear thinkers in America. Or maybe you've tried getting in touch with your feminine side (which you don't have) by acting gentle and talking about your feelings. It's all a waste of time.

Unless you come to God in all your weakness and your complete impotence to ever do anything good or to ever be anything good, you will never come to others as a real man.

We hide our inadequacies because we think they're shameful, abnormal, a reflection of us that's not true of more "together" men. But the exact reverse is true. Masculinity is not the overcoming of neediness; it's the courage to acknowledge neediness and to bring it before God, not to parade it before others in order to be taken care of.

Those are the two mistakes we make. Either we hide our "little boy" fears behind something we think is masculine and mature, or we display our neediness, hoping someone will come through for us. Men who make the first mistake are seen as real men by our culture. Men who commit the second error get labeled as wimps or as effeminate.

The PAPA prayer provides you with a unique opportunity to embrace your worst failures, your most bizarre sexual fantasies, your deepest inadequacies in the presence of God. Start there. It's presenting prayer.

Talk to God. Tell Him what's going on in you when you wake up in a sweat at four in the morning and wonder how you'll ever pay the bills. Express your fear, your shame, your resentment. Pour it all out on God. Be the little boy who needs what you don't have. Embrace your true dependence. When you cried in the middle of the night as a ten-year-old, your dad didn't come. Do it now. Your heavenly Papa will be there.

Then picture who you're talking to. It's God. It's your real Papa, the One who always gets first things in first place and who will help you do the same. He's calling you to be His man, even if you declare bankruptcy or have to confess moral failure. He's touching you on the shoulder, the way He touched a trembling John on Patmos. He's telling you to stand, not as a successful businessman or a respected pastor but as a man, as a man who moves through his world with only one priority: to further God's kingdom. That's attending prayer.

The Spirit will make clear to you how you've reversed values, how you've put second things first, how you think paying your bills matters more than revealing your confidence in God to your wife, how you believe earning respect from others is more satisfying than living to hear His "Well done."

Admit it to God. Call it sin. That's purging prayer. You'll plunge deeper into helplessness. You'll feel like an infant boy, not even a toddler. You can't do anything but depend.

Then you'll come, in approaching prayer, to God. You'll believe more deeply than you've ever believed before that without God, you really can't do anything of real value (John 15:5). You can act cool, get mad, and crack jokes, but you have no power to love, to courageously move into your relationships and circumstances with only one purpose: to please God and reveal Him to others.

So you'll come as a prodigal who longs to be held by your Papa, who dares to hope that He still wants you, that He likes you and is glad, delighted, thrilled you're His son.

"God, I come, weak, burdened, wrong. But I come. As Your helpless son, a little boy who so badly wants to be with his Dad, with a Papa I know is there, with wisdom and strength and all the resources I don't have but that I need to live as a man.

"I count on You to forgive me for depending on everything but You, for thinking I could pull off my life without You. And I trust You to release me from my prison of fear and helplessness into the liberty of the sons of God."

Let the PAPA prayer become your lifestyle, your daily conversation with God. Come as a little boy to your Papa so you can come to others as a real man, a man of uncompromising integrity and unstoppable movement.

A Final Word

$\mathcal{A}t$ no time in history has learning to pray relationally been more important. I see three trends in Western Christianity that make it so.

First, in record numbers, Christians are living for this world and thinking they are living the Christian life. We plan for tomorrow with personal comfort in mind, and we review yesterday with healing from pain as our goal. It's sheer narcissism. It's relating with ourselves, not with God or others, except where it serves our purposes of self-fulfillment, self-promotion, and self-realization.

Second, never before has managerial religion been more plausibly misrepresented as Christ-centered Christianity. And the church is largely blind to its deception. Making things happen, whether growing a church or organizing small-group ministry, has displaced spiritual formation in spiritual community as the real reason we gather together. We gather to achieve a useful purpose, not to meet. Achievement trumps encounter as our primary value. Connecting to share Christ is no longer the point. Reaching goals is the focus. The effect is agenda-driven lives full of cooperation and conflict, devoid of community.

Third, division among Jesus followers, though nothing new, is now dealt with more by principles of conflict resolution and anger management, and less with profoundly spiritual resources. The idea of union with Christ by the Spirit in His tension-free relationship with the Father is dismissed (if it's thought about at all) as religious rhetoric for old-timers. We no longer depend on union with Christ for the power to transform bitter combatants into self-denying saints who love like Him.

We're no longer aware of the desperate need to enter this union by taking seriously our blindness and, in facedown humility, begging the Spirit to let us see our well-disguised self-obsession. Idolatrous attachment to second things, like being treated with respect by others, is no longer even a category to consider. Getting our own way is now a value, not a sin. Unrecognized self-obsession continues to destructively impact other people, whether in church staff meetings or during family dinners.

Our desperate need today is to pray relationally. Relational prayer cuts into narcissism. It focuses our attention on who we are now, where we are now, in the immediate present where eternity intersects our lives, exposes our self-obsession, and draws us into the God-life.

Relational prayer stirs our hunger for real community and makes us dissatisfied with merely functional community, no matter how impressive its achievements. It helps us be before we do, connect before we cooperate.

And relational prayer lifts us high enough to catch a glimpse of the real battle between good and evil; and it lets us see how often we're on the wrong side when we think we're on the right one.

The urgent need of today's church is not better management, more programs, stronger opposition to moral evil in our culture, or a clearer statement of biblical principles to follow in dealing with our lives. We must return to worship as participation by the Spirit in the Son's relationship with the Father. We must return to the Bible as the one book God wrote to reveal who He is, what He's doing in the unseen world, and what His power can do in our hearts.

And we must return to prayer as our opportunity not to get a better life of more blessings now, but to enter more intimately into relationship with God. As one pastor recently said to me, "I've built this church on my giftedness and management ability. Little has happened as a result of my relationship with God. I want that to change."

I offer the PAPA prayer to return the body of Christ, and all its lonely members, to the center of their privileged position, to a close relationship with God. I offer this book to restore prayer to its highest purpose.

Notes

An Invitation to Pray the PAPA Prayer

1. Quoted in J. Oswald Sanders, *Spiritual Leadership* (Chicago: Moody, 1994), 86.

Chapter 5—The Prayer of a Spoiled Child

1. E. Stanley Jones, *365 Days with E. Stanley Jones* (Nashville: Abingdon, 2000).
2. Ravi Zacharias, *Recapture the Wonder* (Nashville: Integrity, 2003), 163.

Chapter 6—Relational Prayer Is About God and Me

1. Quoted in J. Oswald Sanders, *Spiritual Leadership*, 85.

Chapter 8—Stay at Home with Christ

1. Oswald Chambers, *My Utmost for His Highest* (Westwood, N.J.: Barbour, 1935), 140, July 11.
2. I sometimes worry that the current focus in the Christian community on living by desire and finding satisfaction in Christ may be a perversion of Jonathan Edwards's important teaching. He rightly insisted that we are called to be satisfied with God, not merely and stoically submissive. Edwards and his best modern interpreter, John Piper, are correct—God is most glorified in us when we're most satisfied in Him. But more often than we like to admit, that satisfaction is more an article of resolute faith than an experience of happy pleasure.
3. Quoted in James G. S. S. Thompson, *The Praying Christ* (Vancouver, B.C., Canada: Regent College, 1995), 13.

Chapter 12—Stop Trying to Be Who You Think You Should Be

1. In both stories, I've changed names and identifying details. Otherwise, the stories are true.

Chapter 13—Enter Your Red Dot—Don't Just Describe It

1. Lawrence J. Crabb, *God of My Father: A Son's Reflections on His Father's Walk of Faith* (Grand Rapids: Zondervan, 1994).

Chapter 14—Who Do You Think You're Talking To?

1. C. S. Lewis, *The Screwtape Letters* (New York: MacMillan, 1982), all excerpts taken from pages 38–39.

Chapter 15—Who Has God Shown Himself to Be?

1. Darrell W. Johnson, *Discipleship on the Edge: An Expository Journey through the Book of Revelation* (Vancouver, B.C., Canada: Regent College, 2004), 14. I have drawn extensively from Johnson's excellent book in writing this chapter.

Chapter 17—Abandon Yourself to Holiness

1. It might be worth your time now to read Galatians 3:1–5. In that passage, Paul makes it clear that no one is declared holy (justified) because of his or her moral effort; and no one becomes holy (sanctified) by moral effort. Both forgiveness and growth, both acceptance in God's family and maturing as God's children, are works of God.

A Revolution in Relationships

If you would like to journey further, Larry Crabb and NewWay Ministries are dedicated to helping you. Join the many who are excited about spiritual formation and authentic community to help ignite a revolution in how Christians live, think, and relate.

NewWay Ministries (non-profit) seeks to introduce people to this new way and better equip them for living, thinking, and relating in the "new way of the Spirit" that the gospel makes possible (see Romans 7:6).

Our intended contribution to this revolution occurs through three distinct areas :

Conferences
School of Spiritual Direction
Media/Literature

If you would like a list of additional books, products, upcoming conferences, School of Spiritual Direction dates, speaking engagements, or to find out more about NewWay Ministries go to:

www.newwayministries.org

For inquiries please contact us at:

info@newwayministries.org

Our desire is to deepen your awareness of God until knowing Him becomes your greatest hope and revealing Him to others in the way you relate becomes your clearest purpose.

It's time for a Revolution in Relationships, for joining each other's journey through the joys and sorrows of life into the presence of God!

LARRY CRABB'S GROUNDBREAKING WORK OF THE LANGUAGE GOD LONGS FOR US TO SPEAK!

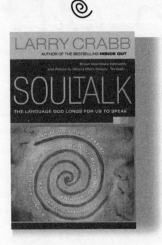

In *SoulTalk,* Dr. Larry Crabb introduces a revolutionary new way for Christians to experience God, a process he calls "soul talk," which happens when two Christians talk to each other in a way that results in their passion for God being stirred, ignited, and released. You'll learn a language that, when used, releases supernatural power that enables you to move to the deepest level of relationships with fellow Christians and with God. The culmination of a lifetime of research and writing, *Soul-Talk* carries a vision for what the church was created to be.

ISBN 1-59145-039-X (hardcover)

ISBN 1-59145-347-X (trade paper)

THOMAS NELSON
Since 1798

For other products and live events,
visit us at: thomasnelson.com

AVAILABLE WHEREVER BOOKS ARE SOLD